I0414939

Contributors

Authored by ~ *Marianne Mooney*

Volume Editors ~ *C. Mooney*

M.D. Mooney

Photographs ~ *Kate Mooney*

Country of Publication   ~ United States

Language ~ English

Primary Category ~ Social Science / Woman's Studies

Title ID   3424613
ISBN: 1450522173
EAN – 13 9781450522175

~ 2010 ~

Stepping out of the Darkness into the Light

A True Story of Abuse Kept Silent

By Marianne Mooney

This is a true story.

The events and situations are all true.

This book is a depiction of cruelty and the emotional ups and downs of an abusive life endured for so very long. The names of the people and places have been changed to preserve the privacy of all those involved.

Although I refer to signs of abuse and methods of control, I do not provide advice to others who may be in a similar situation. This is not a "self-help" book; rather, it is a true story. It mainly reflects the raw hardship of the lives of the abused, their daily struggles to cope, how they finally broke free; and how they continue, today, to attempt to recover from the years of abuse.

Dedicated to:
My daughter, my "Pumpkin"
And
My son, my "Monkey"
I lived for you and you alone.
Protecting and loving you,
for you were the sunshine
in my darkest days.
I loved you then,
And
I shall always love you.

To Moe,
Our guardian angel,
without you we would not
have survived.
You were there through the darkest
of times,
Giving us hope, hugs and a smile,
And, most of all, the love we could always
count on!
To my husband Maurice,
You gave me strength, encouragement and time.
You showed me patience and understanding.
Through it all, you were there
being my friend.
If I could choose one place to always be,
it would be in your loving embrace.
I love you and treasure all that we share together.
Your devoted wife and friend.

CONTENTS

~ ~ ~

Prologue

Turmoil and Darkness Begin Subtly   1

Pushing Buttons   15

Supper   19

Beaten with the Belt   22

Judo   26

Still More Degrading Sex   29

Scouts and Camping   34

Jekyll and Hyde   41

Chores   57

Hide and Seek   62

Counseling   68

Attention and Play Time   73

Mother and Daughter Write   78

Victor's Fault   95

Vehicles and Toys 101

My Personal Pain 106

Day Care and Work 118

Explosive Situation 122

The Separation 129

The Divorce 146

Guilt 154

Tim's Drinking 159

Phone Calls 163

New Directions 170

Kids' Troubles 176

Annulment 179

Still Paying the Price 182

Finally 190

Epilogue

~ *Prologue* ~

I was happy as a kid and a typical tomboy. It was nothing for my twin brother and me to run through the woods barefoot or to shimmy up a tree. Growing up with five brothers and lots of neighborhood boys around, a girl learns to be aggressive, fast, and a fighter. I was all these things and more.

The older boys never left us little kids out of their games. We played "little kids run the bases" (it was a variation of baseball) and we all enjoyed it. There would be a least one batter, a catcher, and a pitcher; whoever was left would cover the rest of the positions. The little kids stood in line eager and ready to run when the ball was hit. Each guy stayed up at bat until three outs were made. Once that happened, the guys would rotate spots and the game would continue with us kids running from base to base. On one occasion, I got clobbered hard between the big boys while running to first base. They sandwiched me right between the two of them, but that did not stop me: I just got up and played some more.

Another time we were playing football in the front yard, my brothers, their buddies and me. I was quite agile and limber as a kid, and also very quick. The ball was snapped and, then, a huge pig pile was created on top of it. Mom yelled out the front door for the boys to get off me. All she saw was the ball, the boys and me. She thought I was plowed under the heap of boys. To her surprise, I yelled from the goal line, "Look at me!" I had grabbed the ball quick and ran with it before anyone knew what happened. I was standing at the goal line laughing, football in hand, while everyone else was in a mound of bodies on the ground.

At parties, I would be the one to instigate water fights. I would take a bucket of water and throw it over the rail onto one of my brothers or douse a cousin with a pitcher of ice-cold water. I always had buckets of water and squirt guns stashed around the yard in preparation for the inevitable water fight. It became a family tradition to throw me into the pool at every party. Even if the pool was just a 'little kids' pool, four-foot round by one-foot deep, in it I would go. To this day, I bring extra clothes with me to all family functions because there is always plenty of water available. Revenge was sweet; everyone knew that if I got wet they would get it back, no doubt about it, but all in harmless fun... laughing, running and playing without a care or a threat - what a joy.

The competitive spirit was always in high gear when I played badminton against my brothers - no rules and no boundaries! With the racket constantly moving between my right and left hands, I would combat the bombardment of birdies smashed over the net towards me. Mom would root for me because I was so little, much younger than the guys, and the only girl gutsy enough to play against the older boys.

I always stayed active and fun-loving, from youth to adulthood. When I was a kid, Mom would often have me show off for the aunts and uncles. I took gymnastic lessons for several years. I would run across the yard doing cartwheels, round-offs and walkovers for all to see. As I got older, I would buy little wind-up toys and send them scurrying across the floor at work to surprise people, or make giant paper airplanes and shoot them across the room. One of these airplanes got caught in a machine and jammed it good. No one squealed on me; in fact, everyone thought it was pretty funny! I laughed, I smiled, I played, and I was happy.

This is not to say that life was all fun - there were hard times. My dad abandoned us when we were young, leaving Mom with seven children - five boys and two girls - and he never supported us. Because none of us have ever seen or heard from him in over 40 years, I don't know today if he is dead or alive. I could pass him every day on the street and not know it was him.

I was six years old when our dad left us. I have only two memories of him. The first involves me getting into trouble. I'd done something wrong and was in the bathroom about to get a spanking; Dad was over me with his tongue curled up and his hand raised. My second, and last, memory of my father was formed on a bright sunny day in the middle of the summer. The sky was a brilliant blue, the trees full with vibrant shades of green and the sun was casting its warm sunshine down on us. We had not seen Dad for a while and missed him a lot. He came walking up the front lawn smiling and waving to us kids. We were so happy and thrilled to see him. We all ran to meet him at once and knocked him over with all our hugs and kisses.

My little brother was four years old when mom started dating. Henry, who had ten children of his own, came to visit one day. He brought one of his sons over with him and, of course, the child called him "Dad." My little brother, who was only three months old when our father left, turned to Mom with deep questioning eyes and asked, "Mom, what is a "dad?" How sad. The other child had called his father, "Dad," but that was a word that my brother had never heard because we had no one to call "Dad." Years later, Mom married Henry.

We hated him at first. Henry was just like Archie Bunker: mean, rude, hard-headed, and he liked his beer. The seven of us were not allowed in each other's rooms, and Heaven help any of us if we talked back to him. I remember Henry literally kicking one of my older brothers around the yard for mouthing off to him. He had my brother by the back of the shirt and was kicking him in the backside with his booted foot, all the while yelling at him. Henry and my oldest brother got into a fistfight at the top of the stairs one evening. Mom, who, after major surgery, had just returned from the hospital only a few days before, came crawling up the stairs hunched over in pain to try to stop them from beating each other. This really made an impression on me - despite Mom's physical condition, she was going to try to stop the abuse from taking place.

Often times, Henry's abuse was of the emotional kind. I remember that once we had gone to visit some relatives and were just getting ready to leave. Mom was looking for me and asked Henry where I was. He replied that he didn't care where I was, *that I wasn't his daughter.* I was crushed. Even though we didn't show much affection towards each other, I had thought that he cared about me - but he didn't. My older brothers finally moved out because they could not stand to be in the same house with him. After my twin brother left the house because of Henry, Mom said to me, "Don't you ever let him force *you* to leave this house, too." And even though it was hard to watch his abuse, I did stick it out, finally leaving the house when I got married.

But I was still feeling good in those days. Even though, for example, I never quite measured five feet in height - always four feet, eleven inches tall - that didn't stop me from driving a great big, dark green Ford LTD. I couldn't quite reach the pedals, so Henry put extensions on the gas and brake pedals for me (yes, they do make extensions for the pedals!). And at about that time of my life, I absolutely loved bowling;

Saturday night was bowling night for me! Off I would go, by myself, in my great big car to the bowling alley. I had a lot of friends there, and some of the guys would hit on me; but that didn't bother me because I knew my mind and had control. And because I thought of myself as invincible, I did do a *very stupid* thing one night after bowling. We had just finished a bowling tournament, so a bunch of us were going out after for drinks. I didn't need a ride; I had my car and could drive myself. So, off we went. I had had two drinks, but being small and not a drinker, that's all it would take for me to feel good. After a few hours of partying, I drove myself home. **Not** a smart thing to do, but I was overly courageous and didn't fear anything. I was free and felt I could do whatever I wanted.

But this sense of invincibility, although strong, was, once again, seriously put to the test when a relative molested my sister and me. He told us that if we said anything to Mom or anyone else, that Mom would hate us and think badly of us. So what could a frightened little girl do, but keep her mouth shut and bury the ugly truth? I just had to become stronger. Too, I once had a boyfriend who would punch me - but I was still a fighter then and would pound him back to let him know that he was not going to get away with abusing me. With all that I endured throughout my childhood, I still had "me" inside: I was happy, had self-respect, and was a daredevil and a damn good hard fighter. Nothing could beat me down growing up. I had strength and courage, determination and will power; that's what I was made of. No boxes to hide in and no darkness to claw my way out of, head held high with strength of mind to get through each day - no matter what was dealt to me.

Then I got married. As time went on, Tim (my husband) slowly drained all the life out of me and all the strength and determination that used to be part of my being. *And so my story begins...*

1. *Turmoil and Darkness Begin Subtly*

The violence, the emotional scaring, the fear, the anguish and embarrassment: it was mine and mine alone, and alone I had to be silent. If people knew what went on they would think less of me and discard me like rubbish. I remembered the rules I was given when molested as a child! *Keep quiet!* My former feelings of worth no longer existed; I did not deserve to be happy. MY role was to be keeper of the house and the deeply hidden, dark secrets that lurked within its walls. Acknowledgment did not belong in my world, I felt if I acknowledged what was truly happening, my world would be destroyed. Depression was my companion. My reality existed in a black abyss where I struggling to survive, clawing my way out, but with no light to guide me. Spinelessness was mine for the taking and keeping: tension, fear and sadness were what I was now made of. Always on edge, jumping on demand, cowering and shaking. This was how my days were filled. Not strength, but weak was my makeup.

Like a rug, I lay there while being beaten and stepped on over and over again. These are the things I knew well and well I did, but in my heart deep within me there *were* hopes and dreams. I was cunning and battled my way to the top of that abyss for what seemed like an eternity. I finally saw the light and gripped it with all that was inside of me. I came to *know* that I would survive and become the person I was always meant to be.

My children and I (Samantha is my name; Marti, my daughter, is the older child; and my son, Victor, the younger) were in an abusive situation for 19 years. We survived, but not without a lot of tears, fear and *not* without significant long-lasting pain and heartache. Throughout my marriage, I never thought I was a strong person, but after looking back through the eyes of therapy and hearing my therapist tell me." Look at what you have been through and are going through now. You are stronger than you realize and have been all along. You just didn't know it."

Abuse is very demeaning, whether physical, mental, verbal or sexual. I was an emotional wreck. It starts subtly and continues to grow. Little by little I was put down. I didn't do things correctly or in the time allotted to me. I was not organized, not smart enough, not good enough, and not fast enough - no matter how hard I tried. "What are you stupid, can't you do anything right?" I didn't know it was happening until it was too late. Ever so slowly I started to feel worse and worse about myself and what I would attempt to do. No matter what I did it wasn't right. Over time I had become worthless without realizing it was happening. Without the abusing spouse I felt I didn't stand a chance in the world, because he had me believing that I couldn't survive without him.

He threatened to take away the children and let me know, in no uncertain terms, everyone and everything would be against me if I didn't keep silent. He was always so critical of everything I did. I hurt more each time, there was no respect and he did not cherish me as a person, but I was kept as one of his possessions, *isolated* and *alone.*

Conversation was of no use because no matter what I said it was wrong and then I would feel worse than before. No matter what I said, he did not listen and it was not to his liking and did not fit logically into his scheme of things. There was no escape; no one to talk to and nowhere to go. He wanted me to talk to him, tell him what was going on. But, when I did it was not what he wanted to hear and it fell on deaf ears so, after a while, *I just stopped talking.*

Depression set in, numb and without feeling; I went through the motions of everyday *living.* Walking in a stupor with deadened mind just nothingness. Then I was sitting on a swing without the slightest hint as to how I got there. Through blank bleak eyes I sat staring out into the world with nothing but absolute and total sadness engulfing me. It terrified me. I was losing my mind, no control; not even over my own self and mind. I could not remember the strong courageous child of the past. My frustrations were taken out on the children. I couldn't help it, yelling all the time because it was my only "out" of the misery I was living. Even though I was frustrated I knew that I must protect my children. I couldn't yell at Tim so I yelled at my children. I didn't want to but it happened. I never hit them because they got enough of that from Tim. They didn't deserve to be used as a punching bag. They didn't do anything to get what was dished out to them. As bad as I felt, I had to go on, because their lives depended on me, no matter what.

Tim was always angry and bitter so I could never let my guard down. He put me down to make himself feel better and superior, to be the big man, to be the big shot. He had total *Power and Control*. A life partner is *supposed* to help you grow, but he held me back, kept hammering me back into the ground until I had no way out. Only darkness surrounded me. The light faded, got dimmer and dimmer. There was no insight to guide me. With each breath I took the darkness continued to surround and suffocate me. I could not breathe.

Just maybe it wasn't about me. Maybe it was really all about him and his own insecurities. Maybe Tim (the abuser) should have been accountable for things he said and did, and not me! He picked on me to make himself feel better. He even had me compromise myself and what I believed in for his own ego. He made our home a battle ground, not the safe place to land or the soft place a person wanted to be. So after 19 years of marriage I did the hardest thing I ever had to do. I stood up to him; I told him I no longer loved him and then told him to leave.

We met in fifth grade; we were in the same grade and classroom. Children that age, fifth – sixth grade are just starting to notice each other. Girls are giggling in the coatroom about the cute boy in the front row and boys are on the playground talking about the cute girls that sit across from them in the classroom. Tim and I noticed each other. We talked a little, but like most children that age boys and girls have cuties, and you are not supposed to talk to them or the other children will tease you. So we went our own way and met again in high school, tenth grade.

There was a group of us that hung around together. Tim hung around with my twin brother mostly. After a while; mom would tease him and ask which twin he was there to see.

We dated for a while and then he started seeing someone else, which broke my heart. That was it. I didn't speak a word to him for over two years. Tim went into the service and I got a job. During this time we both got engaged, but it didn't work out for either of us. Having the same group of friends that still hung out together; we would eventually run into each other once again. After a few years we started dating again. He was in the service and he seemed to have grown up. He seemed so sweet and caring, after some time we got engaged.

Tim was so demanding early on, but I didn't see it. I was young and naive and thought I was in love. He wanted sex all the time and me being young thought it was what I was supposed to do, after all we were engaged. He was in the service, and on weekends, when he came home, the first thing he would want was sex. His mom caught us one night. We were in his bedroom when she came in to check on him. She was livid. I heard her stomp down the hall and her voice raised telling Tim's dad what just happened. I was mortified and embarrassed, but Tim still wanted to finish. He was never satisfied. I said no, just take me home. *It was inevitable, I got pregnant.*

We were planning an October wedding, but things had to be moved up. Instead we would be married in April. He came home for Christmas and I hadn't completed the wedding plans that he wanted done. I had been working on a very large detailed latch hook rug wall hanging for him. I wanted it to be done when he got home. He didn't know it was hanging in his room when he got there. He really laid into me about not getting things done for the wedding (another clue that I didn't see his temper). He finally went into his room and was totally surprised to see the ship hanging on his wall. He really liked it and thanked me for it, but never apologized for yelling at me in front of his family.

April finally arrived and we got married. I didn't sleep much the night before. We had a lot of company staying over and my aunt snored all night. Plus I was excited, it was my wedding day. I was going to marry the man I loved and would spend the rest of my life with, share my dreams with and raise my children with. I was told Tim was excited too and that he almost walked out of the house without his pants on. We went to Pennsylvania for the weekend. Tim being in the service couldn't get much time off; so that was our honeymoon. Tim was stationed in Michigan, so after our honeymoon, off to Michigan we went.

I was so nervous. I was leaving my family for the first time and driving on the highways for the first time. Where was my bravery that I remembered? His dad gave Tim the truck that he had always wanted for our wedding gift. I drove Tim's car and he drove the truck. I had never driven on the highway for any length of time. Now I was on the road for over four hours. It was a long nerve racking trip for me trying to keep up with Tim. The truck would become a bone of contention in the future.

Being in the service Tim didn't make a lot of money. I was allowed $50.00 every two weeks for food and that included baby food and diapers once the baby was born. We had a lot of chicken, pasta, tuna and cereal. I decided one night that I would make pancakes for supper. It was cheap and on a tight budget it fit very well.

There were seven children, my mom and no dad growing up so we often had pancakes for supper. It didn't cross my mind that Tim would get upset if I made them for supper. I prepared a nice hot stack of them and had everything ready when he got home. Boy was I wrong! Tim blew his top. He yelled at me, telling me that pancakes were for breakfast not supper and that I had better make him something else (another unseen sign of his abuse). It scared me and I cried because he was yelling at me over a little thing like pancakes. I got up and made something to his satisfaction. Tim's idea of a wife was much like the old saying; keep her at home barefoot and pregnant. When the children were born it didn't surprise me that he never fed them and never changed a dirty diaper. His idea of helping was to wake me up so I could attend to the baby's needs.

Again I saw his temper. We had just returned from visiting his friends on the base. When he got out of the truck he accidentally dropped the keys on the ground. When he got up he hit his head on the mirror of the truck. He got so angry that he balled his hand into a fist and smashed it into the mirror. I flinched and stood there shaking totally shocked that he had done that. The mirror shattered and now his hand was covered with blood. He had cut his knuckles deep. We had to get into the car and drive back to the base where he got stitches.

My being pregnant didn't stop Tim from wanting sex. I would say it hurt or was uncomfortable, but it didn't matter to him. A plain brown package arrived about a month after we were married. He had ordered a pair of crotch less panties and bra set with holes in the top for nipples.

How could a guy presume such a thing for a new and pregnant

life? I was so embarrassed when he had me put it on, because it made me feel dirty and very self-conscious standing there with him leering at me. I realize being newly married there is an adjustment period, but this just wasn't for me. I was not happy, but what could I do. I was alone and had no one to talk to.

We had a loud lengthy argument, so I went for a walk. The woman down stairs mentioned she had heard it and asked if I was okay. It was a gray dreary day out with rain pouring down, but I didn't care. The day fit my mood sad, gray and unsettled. He never came after me to make sure I was all right. I had hoped since I was his wife and pregnant he would be concerned.

The only reprieve I had from sex was when our daughter was born. The doctor said no sex for six weeks. But when that time was over Tim went at it again with no concern for me and no communication. No "love making", just sex, his way. He never had enough and was never satisfied. We moved back to Massachusetts a year and a half later; his hitch in the service was up. He finished four years of active duty but decided to stay in the reserves.

We moved in with his family until we found jobs and a place to stay. I learned where Tim got his controlling and demanding, abusive ways. Living with his family was very tense at times. We stayed in one room. His mom would scream at me often to keep the room picked up. We had a double bed, crib, dresser, all that we owned, and a 15-month-old baby girl, Tim and I in that room with no space to move. Finally his parents agreed to let Marti, the baby, stay in another room. His parents Mr. and Mrs. Dudley (throughout this book I will refer to them as Mr. and Mrs. D. or the grandparents, I had grown up calling them Mr. and Mrs. D. and after we got married never felt comfortable calling them mom and dad or by their first names) had two dogs at the time, a Maltese and a Terrier. The Maltese was very tame and laid back; she would even sleep under the crib when Marti was in it. The Terrier was more aggressive and a little hyper. When Marti went to pet the Terrier one day, the dog snapped at her. All hell broke out. Tim literally picked up the dog and threw it across the room. His sister came out screaming, followed shortly thereafter by their dad. There was a big screaming match between Tim, his sister and their father. Tim yelling threatening to kill the dog if it ever snapped at his daughter again, his sister screaming at him because he could hurt the dog and his father yelling at everyone. The result was Tim and his dad not speaking to each other for a few days, which made it terribly uncomfortable because we all lived under the same roof.

I worked from eight in the morning until four thirty in the afternoon, Monday thru Friday in a factory. It was hard, tiring work. I came home from work one day to find that one of Tim's sisters went next door and picked Marti up at the baby sitters. They really loved her and wanted to spend all the time they could with her which was fine with me.

"Grandma Cammy," a nice old lady that fell in love with Marti while we were in Michigan had given Marti some blocks. When I walked in one of the dogs was chewing on the blocks. I started to say something about the blocks being special but I couldn't finish because that is when Tim's mom started in on me. She scolded me, saying, if I picked up and put things away the dog wouldn't get them. I tried saying I wasn't the one who took them out, that Meg had when she brought Marti in. It didn't matter. My plea fell on deaf ears. By this time we were all yelling and arguing. That is when Mr. D. told Tim to take his wife and kid and get the hell out. We did. We found a place a few weeks later and moved out. Four months under their roof was plenty.

We moved into a townhouse in Hill Pond Village. I got pregnant again, now our son, Victor was on the way. If I had known back then what I know today I would never have had children with Tim. The time spent in Hill Pond was not good. This was when Tim started drinking. He met Moe and Phil at work and became fast friends. (Moe got very close to us that we started calling him Uncle Moe for the children). They would come over to the house after work and start drinking. Some days when I got home they would be well on their way to being drunk. In the morning I would put supper in the crock-pot so when I got home after working and picking up the baby, supper would be ready. When I got home from work my supper would be eaten by Tim and his buddies. When I told Tim about it, he thought it was funny and he and his buddies would laugh. I would then have to prepare something else for Marti and myself.

Phil moved into the village a short time later. He and his wife lived up the top of the hill from us. On one particular day; Tim decided to drive his buddy's motorcycle down the hill to our place. This day they were not laughing. He drove the motorcycle into the side of the building because he was so intoxicated. When I went to see if he was all right he just pushed me away. I told him not to drive it again because he was smashed, but he denied being drunk. He went into the house, got a beer came out, got on the motorcycle in his drunken state and drove back up the hill. He was lucky he didn't get hurt or damage anything. He was in serious denial about the extent of his drinking.

In the beginning of our marriage I was braver and would speak up, but it always fell on deaf ears. On this particular occasion; I made sure Tim heard what I was saying. It was near Christmas and Marti had asked when we would get a Christmas tree. Her father told her we would get one when it snowed. To our surprise the next morning there was plenty of snow on the ground. A storm came in overnight and covered everything with at least six inches of snow. Marti's little face lit up like the Fourth of July she was so excited seeing all the snow. Everything was covered in a brilliant white sheen sparkling in the sunshine. The ground crunched underfoot and the air was cold and crisp. I told him he made a promise to our precious little girl and that he was going to keep it. We went out that day and got a big artificial tree for her. She loved it. That night Uncle Moe came over, we had pizza and then the four of us put up her tree together. Marti was so excited choosing ornaments and putting them in just the right spot on the tree. I can still picture her beautiful little face sparkling with laughter and joy so many years ago. Her eyes twinkled with delight and happiness back then.

Our son was born in April. Tim was so proud to have a son but still didn't do much with either of the children. It was a woman's place to clean and take care of the children. Now I had two children I loved with all my heart, a full time job and a husband that wouldn't help with the house or children, was controlling and demanded sex all the time. If he didn't get his way or felt his proverbial "box" closing in on him he would threaten to leave.

This is the first of many letters, journal and diary entrees that you will read throughout this story. The letters and entrees are not corrected for grammar, spelling, and punctuation. They will show the emotional and confusing times we endured and how our lives were in such chaos that we could not put down many complete or coherent thoughts.

A letter from Tim

Hi Hon,

These are some of my thoughts about us. First of all, I think *I've been kind of selfish; reason being is that I should never threaten to leave you.* I've realized these past two weeks that it was just *something I could hold over your head* and *make you do what I wanted.* I've realized this two week that I could never live without you. My life would never be complete. It's funny how being alone can really make you think about life and its relationships.

It must be true; absence makes the heart grow fonder. I didn't realize how my life as it is meant to me. My family, job and security of it all. Your part of my life and nothing will ever change that. Not me, not you or anyone else.

We've both got to talk things out from now on we need that. ***The first thing*** I want to understand is your feelings on sex. I really want to get together on this because we need better relationship there. I've got to learn to read you better on what you like and what *you like to do to me.* I think if we talked to each other while we were doing it we'd know what each was going through. Please tell your feelings on this thing I want to know. I think we've got to talk about our attitude in general toward each other. What we dislike about each other what we like. Maybe when something we do we should tell the other person whether we like or not. And I mean the little things.

What do you think about me wanting you home when I get home? I really want your opinion on that. I just like you home because I really like the feeling of coming home to someone instead of an empty house. I did that for a little over 2 ½ years and it was lonely.

Is there anything else you have that you want to straighten out? Anything else? I just hit on a few things (main-things) that I think if we talk them over we could have a better relation. There could be a hell of a lot more and I want you to bring them up and out into the open. I think it's better this way.

Well now I feel better and I hope this will help us. We can talk this over some more later or whenever you want.

Love ya,

Always & Forever

Tim

P.S. Please don't get mad at any of this thank you!!

Reading this letter now, makes me sick. He wanted to talk over a few main points; the only one I read was about sex and what he wanted me to-do to him. I was totally disgusted with it and it makes me want to throw up. Even this early in our marriage he had control, he said it himself. Threatening me, saying he would leave me in order to control me. Although he said what I wanted mattered, it didn't. I wish I had seen the signs, and then maybe my children and I would not have gone through 19 years of hell from an abusive man. Sure he was saying what I wanted to hear. Let's talk it over, but he never listened and he never heard, because if he did he wouldn't be asking it again. He would know what was bothering me and what I liked and did not like. He was so into himself; of course, he wanted to make me feel better, make me think it was what I wanted: that way, he could keep the manipulation going in the direction he wanted it to go in.

Hi Hon,

How's your day going? Mine are going pretty fast; hopefully the rest of the week goes just as quick. I'm supposed to be studying my course, but I haven't been able to concentrate since our phone call. It seemed like we were so far apart. Do you think there's something wrong with us and if so what is it? I'm really "SICK" confused right now. I really think we should get away for a weekend. Just the two of us and discuss everything out. Maybe when I get back we'll take off by ourselves and talk okay!!

When I get home maybe I'll take the Monday off and we can spend the time together. Have you had your friend yet? If so, you'd better start taking the pill. I'm going to try to make everything right when I get home. We really need to talk everything out. Our communication is going right down the drain. That's what happened to us before.

I sure miss you and the children. I hate to go home because Marti's not there to meet me. And nobody to meet me afterward with a kiss (meaning you). Hopefully Victor's doing better today. If he's anything like Marti, he'll be all right. I hope you feel better too! I bet you got some sleep.

Dad and I did the laundry today. I didn't realize there was that much. Oh, and by the way, you put the seam in the wrong place on my pants. They go down the sides not the middle. You got one part right, you did them inside out. Nobody noticed, but tonight when I tried to iron them out it wouldn't come out. Maybe you'll have better luck. Or maybe I better bring them to the cleaners. Thank – you for remembering the medals I thought I forgot them.

Well kiddo I think it would be a good idea if I closed this letter before it becomes a book. If you get to the mailbox before I get home you'll get the letter before I get home.

I love you and miss you very much. Please give the children a kiss and hug for me.

Love ya

Always & Forever

Tim (daddy)

P.S. Hopefully next week goes by as quick as this week does. Please be home when I get home on Father's Day I really want to see you, I miss you a lot. I really think time has helped us both.

Little signs that I missed would have told me to get out early, but I didn't know any better and didn't see the signs when they happened. Sex of course, did you get your friend yet, you better get on the pill. That only tells me that he wants sex when he gets home. That is his way of spending time together (supposedly talking). And then the critical remarks, so subtly, so little but they all add up after a long time until I believed I couldn't do anything right. His commented about not putting the seams in the correct place on his pants. If he were so worried about our relationship I would think that he would not care about mentioning seems to me. Just a little put down this time but so many more occurred throughout the marriage. He said the communication had broken down before and that this has happened before. He never listened; it was all about him and what he wanted. Oh, he was good with the words, saying again what I wanted to hear, but his actions were totally different.

Every time we moved it was always getting closer to his folks. This time we lived about a mile away. Sex continued to get worse for me. Tim constantly made demands of me. Time and again he was told it hurt and was uncomfortable, but he said I just didn't want it and he would continue. Early on I learned to fake orgasm just to get it over with. It was a chore for me nothing exciting or remotely romantic about it ever occurred.

Tim would go away for work and bring me gifts. Listening to other women speak of husbands trips away and gifts brought home, it would be in my mind that my husband would bring home a nice knickknack, jewelry or something sweet for me. Not Tim, whenever he brought something home for me, it had to do with sex. Usually some kind of dirty, slinky trashy outfit to wear that would enhance sex for him. These all made me feel more and more dirty. It was dreaded times him coming home because I knew what he had in store for me. More contaminated sex, something to make me feel small and filthy. It was like a disease growing increasing in pain and filth. Festering until one day it would destroy all in its wake.

I made friends with the neighbor next door. We met by my throwing a snowball against her kitchen window. She came out; we introduced ourselves and became friends. Sally was a hoot; we called her the "crazy kook." We had lots of fun together. She was a small light of sunshine for me in the few years we lived next to each other. We often played pranks on each other and spent time together with our children. One summer day she hung her laundry out to dry, but she couldn't figure out why it was not drying. She finally figured it out when she saw me with the hose. I had been spraying her laundry all day; so by late afternoon it was still soaking wet.

Another time, I put soda bottles up and down her cellar stairs; we had adjoining cellars. I had forgotten all about placing the bottles on the stairs. About a week later she came over laughing and told me that the meter reader had to go down cellar. That was a bit of a problem because there were bottles on every step going down to the basement. Sally explained to her about our pranks. The woman laughed and kicked the bottles out of the way as she went down to the basement. Sally was a trusting person. She gave me the keys to watch her place when she and her family went on vacation. She laughed like crazy when she got home. I had hard-boiled all her eggs, and glued her sneakers to the kitchen floor. She would get me back, all in fun though. Sally barricaded me into the house using the trashcans. She would jam them into the doors so that they could not be opened. I would have to crawl out the window to remove the cans in order to open the doors. Another time she took what seemed like miles of rope, crisscrossing it throughout the entire cellar. No one could walk without getting caught up in the tangle of rope. She would also give my children ice-cream cones through the hole in the screen of our adjoining porches. Of course they loved that. It took me a while to figure out why the children didn't want to each lunch. She was starting a new at home job selling clothes. I went over one night to check out what she had. We had a good time looking at everything, whether we thought it was out of style or not. We had some wine that night and when I went home I was happy. But that didn't last long.

Tim as usual wanted sex. He had been talking about anal and oral sex for quite some time. That night he took advantage of me. He said I was real loose and he had no trouble having anal sex with me. It was against my will. The next day I felt so violated, unclean and betrayed. I hurt and was ashamed of myself for drinking and not having control, letting him once again get the better of me. Stupid, stupid, I should have known better than to drink. I didn't have much, because I am not a drinker. Never was and never would be. I knew I had to keep my wits about me for the sake of the children and myself. How could my husband do that to me knowing that I absolutely did not want that kind of sex? Knowing he hurt me and that it was uncomfortable for me. That is all he wanted from me from that time on. Refusing over and over again, this caused many arguments between us. I didn't like it, it was unnatural for me, it hurt and he was much too big for me. He should have respected me, but he didn't.

We moved again in two years. This time we moved two houses away from his parents, only one house between us. I really didn't have a say in buying the house. Tim came home one day and said that Dan and Kim the owners were moving and he wanted that house. I knew we could not afford it, but he insisted. It had three bedrooms, living room, and kitchen, breeze way and a two and a half car garage, which Tim really wanted. We worked all kinds of hours getting money together for a down payment. Six months later we were in the house. It was okay at first. His mother tried to help us settle in, making many suggestions as to how things should be set up to her liking. I could understand she had more experience setting up a house, but I wanted my belongings set up my way, it was my house. I needed to have something of my own even if it was only the way the silverware was set up in a drawer. The neighbor living in between us was a good friend to us all. Our back yards looked onto each other. So with their yard in-between us it became as ours. One big yard for the children to cross over and see their grandparents... the children loved it. The newness wore off and we all minded our own business for the most part. If his father did anything for Tim, Tim owed him forever. Tim borrowed money to buy mag wheels for the truck and for years even after it was paid back he still owed his father. His father always threw it in his face. Anything they did for us, we always had to pay back with blood, so to speak. When the money was paid back or the favor was done, it still wasn't over. Tim would never admit it, but I believe that in his mind he could never live up to his father. It would only add to his dissatisfaction with his own life in addition to us, as he perceived it. Tim's controlling ways had started to develop in earnest and living this close to his parents did not help our situation. We paid for it dearly. Tim started to take his frustrations out on us more and more; physically, emotionally, verbally and sexually on me. The house of darkness and tension was slowly starting to develop. It was like a pot of water on the stove; ever so slowly, simmering, on the rise, waiting to erupt with devastation once its boiling point was met.

2. *Pushing Buttons*

In the first few years of marriage I knew how to make that pot boil. I would be so fed up with his treatment of us that I would deliberately get Tim mad at me. That way he could get mad all he wanted and not take it out on the children, or so I thought. Pushing his buttons was the only thing I had to fight back with. There weren't many just a few that actually worked. I knew what the outcome would be if too many buttons were pushed. His temper would flare, the bomb would explode and ultimately a fist would be swung. The children and I would pay a high price even if unknowingly a switch did get pushed. As the years went on, I was no longer able to push his buttons. I finally had no spine left and no energy to fight back with. I knew how to push his buttons before I became spineless. He hated to be called a "Jerk" and that is what I would call him. That is what he was, a great big controlling "Jerk." It was a little way to get under his skin. He would yell at me and declare that he was not a jerk and that I better not call him that again. But I would once in a while just the same. The day I really thought he was going to smash my face in for calling him a "Jerk" was the last time I did. Tim was instantly violent, angry, and turned on me. I stood riveted to my place, eyes wide with shock and shook with fear as he came at me. He got in my face. His teeth gritted, red face and threatened me. One hand was fisted tight and the other; that jabbing pointed finger warning me never to call him a "Jerk" again. Television was another button I could push. Of course with him wanting sex all the time, I would dread going to bed. So now I would watch TV, even if I wasn't really into the show I would make believe that I was and that I wanted to see the outcome. He would get so mad at me for not wanting to go into the bedroom with him. It was a way to get back at him and most of all a way to get out of having sex with him. He would go into the bedroom saying he was stood up for the stupid TV and slam the door. I knew the children would not get into trouble because they were already in bed and were safe for the time being.

We both had pools growing up and knew it would be fun if we had one. We decided to buy one, but had not decided where to put it. I wanted it over to the side of the yard so it could be fenced off, that way we would still have a good size yard for the children to play in. I came home from work one hot summer day to find that Tim and Uncle Moe had started the groundwork for the pool right in the middle of the yard, right off the patio in-between three trees. It was a 27 - foot round pool and took up a lot of space, which split the yard into two smaller sections. He wanted it there and that was that. I had no say in the matter.

Tim had always been hot headed, so I learned early on that if he was in the middle of doing something don't let anything else get in the way of it being finished. If I did make a suggestion he would ignore it or blow his stack. Heaven help anyone or anything that would obstruct what he was trying to accomplish. The day we installed the pool was pure hell for all of us. I didn't dare push any buttons for all of our sakes. He was in such a black mood no one dared step out of line. With his temper came the pervasive. We would all be uneasy and walk on eggshells, because we didn't know if or when his temper would go off.

He was like a rattlesnake poised and ready to strike in an instant, keeping constant vigil over his possessions and territory; taking out the opposition to maintain control. We were putting up the sides of the pool and having a hard time. Tim's black mood was getting blacker. Things were not going well and he was getting extremely mad and irritated. I could tell he was trying to keep himself under control as other people were around. He didn't want to lose it in front of others and make himself look like a fool and idiot. Everyone was on edge because of it. It was hot and taking a lot longer than he had planned. The neighbors and our family had been at it for hours.

I was always barefoot in the summer and this day was no different. As we struggled to put up the sides I slipped and sliced my big toe on the runners that were to hold up the sides of the pool. I let out a small, quiet whimper because of the pain and then saw the blood darken the dirt as it started to sink into the ground. My friend looked at me when she heard my cry. She told me to go clean it up and bandage it. But, I knew if I left my post I would be in horrible trouble later, if not in front of everyone. Tim would put me down, and let me know how dim-witted he thought I was for not wearing shoes and for causing more delay in putting up the pool. Tim would without a doubt be pissed off that I cut my toe. He would make me believe it was to stop, a day wasted because of me. I shook my head "no" at her and said I would be okay. I said nothing and kept working on the pool with everyone else. I worked with blood covering my toes and the ground. I stood on. My fear of his wrath and his unreasonable expectations kept me in pain as the dirt caked up inside my cut, throbbing and burning. We worked for hours getting the sides set. It was late and everyone was grubby hot and sweaty when we finally finished. Tim ordered pizza for everyone. I was grateful for that, because we were all exhausted, grimy and on edge. While we waited for the pizza to arrive, I went into the bathroom to clean my foot. It was now filthy black, covered with dried blood and the cut was now encrusted with dirt. I cleaned and cleaned it, crying, wincing in pain, scrubbing it till the dirt was completely eliminated then bandaged it and went out to join the others. The cut was about an inch long and deep. I don't know if I needed stitches, because by the time I got to clean it out, it had stopped bleeding. It was very painful. I was lucky that it didn't get infected. For a few days it was hard to walk on it, because of the pain and swelling. The whole time just thinking I can't let Tim know or I would get in trouble for being "stupid" and causing a problem for him. I never told Tim about the cut. He never knew it was in my best interest not to tell him. There were a lot of things he never knew. I feared his anger and reactions, so I didn't tell him.

To my astonishment, the next day he picked up the children from the sitter. He and Uncle Moe finished putting in the liner and were filling the pool. The children were happily running around, playing and splashing in the crystal clear water as the pool filled up on this beautiful sunshiny day.

It was not until years later that I learned that most people came over to make it easier on the children and me. They knew that if they were around that Tim would ease off on us for awhile. They wanted to make sure that we were okay and knew that Tim was more likely to keep himself in check with other people around. Most times we paid dearly after everyone left if things went wrong, especially Victor. Looking back, it's clear to me that people knew; I just didn't realize at the time that it was so obvious to others.

A few days later, Tim decided to throw me into the pool. The water was ice cold and he knew I hated cold water. After he threw me in, he told me to get out and go change. He said he was able to see through my shirt. It was a light peach colored shirt and there was only the slightest hint of my nipples showing through. Since I was already in, I refused to get out. I played with my children and Uncle Moe for at least an hour. Tim stood in the pool with his arms crossed over his chest just glaring at me he was extremely angry. I wasn't getting out even though I was freezing because I knew it was getting to him. I was going to get back at him for throwing me in the pool. It felt wonderful to be having a great time with my children and their uncle knowing he was mad. Yet, as I played and laughed with my children and their uncle, dread filled me for I knew I was in horrendous trouble for pushing his button and not doing what I was told. Tim let me know in no uncertain terms later what I had done. How dare I embarrass him in front of Uncle Moe and how dare I expose myself in front of him and the kids. He warned me; I better not ever defy him again.

3. Supper

My job was in a factory. The hours I worked, were from 8:00 am until 4:30 pm, Monday thru Friday. It was hard tiring work; running machines all day and heavy lifting that would often result in cuts on my hands. It was up to me to get the children up, dressed, fed and off to the baby sitter, who lived next door, before leaving for work. After work I picked them up, went home and got supper ready. Most times Tim got out of work before me, but he would not pick up the children or start dinner. If he did pick them up; which was rare, I heard all about it; that it was nothing but a pain and inconvenience for him. He couldn't be bothered to pick up his own children and spend some quality time with them. Of course, when I got home the children wanted my attention, which I could not give to them or dinner would be late. Tim always wanted meat, potatoes and vegetables for supper. If he wasn't in the mood for what I prepared he would throw a fit, screaming and hollering at me. I would then have to prepare something else to his liking. Because of Tim's demanding ways, I always tried to have a variety of choices available for dinner. If we had pasta, I would also have vegetables, salad and bread with it. If we had mashed potatoes there would be two types of vegetables along with it.

My son, Victor would literally gag on spaghetti sauce or mashed potatoes because he didn't like them. He would be given plain white spaghetti with butter or extra corn instead of potatoes. He wasn't being a brat as his father called him or just giving me a hard time. He truly didn't like them. Tim however, would insist he eat everything that was prepared.

Tim being the power seeker would insist he eat it and Victor would gag or get sick. Tim would then smack Victor's face or head yelling at him for "acting up." Victor vomited, this one time, and Tim told him to eat it. I jumped up and said that was not going to happen. Victor was sent to his room and grounded forever as usual. Since I stepped in, Tim would be so angry he would go into Victor's room and beat him. Then he would start on me yelling at me not to interfere. I told him he didn't need to pound on Victor and scream at him, he is only a little child and he didn't deserve such treatment. He was only three or four at the time.

All the children got from Tim, was negative attention. Victor picked up on this and figured that was the way it was supposed to be. So he started to deliberately get under Tim's skin all the time. He wanted his father's attention and to spend time with him. He didn't care how he got it as long as he did. Marti was always quiet, not saying much. She just sat looking scared saying nothing, keeping it all in over and over again. If she did say something, Tim would poke her hard in the chest with his finger, yell at her, tell her not to talk back and to straighten out or she would get it again. If Tim didn't like the fork he was given, he would throw it across the room and yell at Marti to get him a different one. Marti knew after his tantrums and pokes in the chest, that she better put the proper fork down the first time. Even simple little thing he had to control.

According to "Tim's law"; pancakes were the only item I absolutely could not make for supper. I made that mistake very early in our marriage. As the years went on, Tim started to go away more frequently for work. One night I asked the children what they wanted for supper. They wanted pancakes. We had pancakes, eggs, ham, toast, bacon and all the breakfast items we had in the house for supper.

I made Mickey Mouse pancakes, teddy bear pancakes, rainbow pancakes, chocolate chip pancakes and the kid's initials for pancakes. We would have pancakes and all the fixings to go with it when he went away. We truly enjoyed it and looked forward to the next time he would go away. In retrospect, I think we were celebrating his absence. We celebrated our stomachs being free of stress. One weekend my daughter had a friend spend the night and we made pancakes. I forgot about the butter and it melted. I put out a basting brush with it for the girls to use to paint the pancakes with the butter. All her friends talked about the painted pancakes. After that, whenever she had a friend over, which wasn't very often, I had to make pancakes for them to paint with melted butter. We found ways to have a little fun.

When Victor was five it was time for him to go to kindergarten. Learning his name and address was a big thing and his father wanted him to know his full name and know it perfectly. Every night at supper time, Tim would ask Victor what his full name was. Victor had to say, "Victor James Dudley is my full name" if he didn't say it properly, Tim would smack him in the head and make him say it over and over again, every night the same thing. Victor would sit there shaking and his little lip would be trembling because he knew what was coming. Victor what is your full name? "Victor James Dudley is my full name." If he didn't say it, a slap in the head, face or mouth.

Supper was not a happy family time for us. It became a dreaded time. It was only a dream to be able to talk and have a nice family dinner together. Sometimes Victor would be sent to bed without his supper, but with a fat lip. That was not fair. He was only a little kid just learning many new things. More and more I would sneak in crackers, or a slice of bread and butter, so he wouldn't be hungry. Gee! It sounds just like prison. It felt like it lots of times. What could we do? There was no way out, no escaping Tim's punishments. Who knows what we did to deserve what was delivered by the hand of a complete and total control freak, my husband, their father. You do what you have to do in order to survive, especially for the children. How can a father get so mad at a little child for not saying his name right? Questions all the time questions, I couldn't understand how my family deserved this treatment. It was just saying his name right; I didn't understand the reasoning behind his logic. What logic is there behind smacking your child in the head? Yes a child needs to know his name but hurting him just makes him feel bad and intimidates him therefore causing more fear and inability to articulate his name upon command. Over and over again my heart went out to my children seeing the look on their faces. Fear and complete bewilderment of the situation was so evident. Most times they didn't know what they did to deserve the slap that was given to them. Their red faces, swollen lips and broken hearts and spirits defied understanding.

4. Beaten with the Belt

It was a beautiful day, the sun shining brightly with blue skies above. But inside the house, our house the ever-looming darkness was once again bearing down upon us with vengeance. My precious little boy, blonde hair, brown eyes, cutest little nose and smile and weighing about 35 - pounds was only four years old. My son, Victor once again at the mercy of his sick, sick father. So vivid still today, twenty years later are the bruises and welt marks on my son's little body after the heinous beating he received from his father. The wickedness and cruelty that was thrust upon him by his father on this day is still so very inconceivable and unimaginable for a small boy to have suffered. Etched forever in my mind, I will never forget the hideousness of what Victor had to tolerate for so many dark miserable years. I have no recollection of what Victor did wrong but his father was livid. It was early evening; Tim was yelling at Victor and ordering me, yet again, to butt out. I knew without a shred of doubt that whatever Victor had done, couldn't have been something so terrible that he deserved to be brutally beaten. In Tim's eyes he really didn't need to have a reason to beat Victor. I remember pleading with him not to hit him. *Please Tim, DON'T!! He is only a little boy!! You're going to hurt him!! Please Tim not again!* His venomous comment, "That's right, a mama's boy," and he pushed me aside.

Once again Victor was fraught with fear. He was shaking as his father who at 5' 8" tall and about 175 pounds towered over him. Violently, Tim shoved Victor into his room and demanded that he pull down his pants. As Tim closed the door I saw him unbuckle his belt and remove it. I stood frozen as I heard the force with which the belt came down over and over again on my little boy's bare bottom and legs. I cried and cried as I stood there shaking wondering what my son would look like. Little did I know at the time that it was not so much what he would look like, but rather the effect it would have on his self esteem and emotional scars it would leave years later? All I wanted to do was rush in there and save him, but I couldn't. My arm wouldn't reach out and turn the knob I was paralyzed with fear. His father's rage would grow instantaneously and the beating would become viler if I "meddled." I stood there with sweat running down my back, tears streaming down my face, shaking listening to the whack of his belt on my little son. Flinching each time the belt made its mark, crying for my son. The sound over and over again, the whistle of the belt through the air, then the impact on my son the slapping crack of leather on bare skin and his screams crying in total despair; nothing I could do but wait it out and hope my precious boy would be okay. I stood as if my feet were nailed to the floor. It was my fault. It was always my fault for not keeping the children in line and for not being a good mother and wife. I wish I had been a stronger person; I could have helped my son. God, why couldn't anyone help us? Why was this happening to us? Why were we so alone? There was only one word that could describe what I felt for Tim and that was I *despised* him. Marti would disappear into her room, when this happened, afraid she was next. At six years old, she would be curled up on her bed shaking wondering why this was happening. Tim came out of the room still in a rage. Now it was my turn.

He wouldn't hit me, but he was screaming and yelling at the top of his lungs furious. He was degrading and threatening me as always. It didn't matter what he said to me all I wanted to do was get to my son, but he wouldn't let me. He was yelling, "Mama's boy doesn't need you. Stop babying him". Only after persistent pleading, he would finally allow me to go to my son. Victor was sitting on his bed frantically shaking, hands on his knees, crying, tears streaking down his cheeks. His precious little face twisted in pain, little lips quivering tormented. I stared at that broken little person for a moment, my heart breaking once again into a million pieces and cried more tears, tears of sorrow and great pain for my dear sweet child, then hugged him and put him to bed where I prayed he would be safe from his father. The man who should love, comfort and protect him.

Again, Victor wasn't allowed out of his room to have supper. I knew he wouldn't dare leave his room, so later I quietly snuck into his room and brought him some crackers. He nibbled the crackers quickly for we both knew, if caught, all hell would break out once again. He flinched with each move and still sobbed from the assault. It was quite evident he was in immense pain and suffering. I could only imagine the pain he was enduring because of the abusive attack his father inflicted upon him.

The next day when I looked at Victor, I couldn't believe the bruises on his tiny 35 - pound body. Raised welts so black and blue covered his legs and butt. It was unbelievable that his father could do such a contemptible thing to a beautiful little boy. Marks inches wide and six inches long if not longer. My fear was absent and instead I was furious. My backbone would come forth once in a while and on this day I was enraged. I cried and screamed at Tim, "How could you?" I yelled at him and swore at him and warned him; don't ever do it again. All he said, "don't chastise me and don't interfere or he'll get it worse." He didn't show any signs of remorse or regret for what he did to that little boy. What a despicable brute. What a poor excuse for a man, a husband, a father. I kept Victor in long pants for a week to hide the nasty bruises covering his body. It terrified me that someone would find out, report the bruises and that he'd get taken from me. He needed to know that at least his mommy loved him even if I couldn't protect him from a demonic person.

On the following weekend we went to a picnic in Vermont. It was Memorial Day and there was always a huge family gathering. All the relatives from Massachusetts showed up as well as everyone that lived in Vermont. I could let my guard down for a short time. With so many people around Tim would be the perfect gentleman all-day, loving, caring and kind. He would show the sweet side that was never present in our house of doom and gloom. There was lots of food, drinks and games to play, plenty of activity for everyone. The children had a ball all day. They were so filthy and happy for a change, running, playing tag with their cousins and laughing. What a beautiful sight to behold, smiles and shining faces in the bright sunshine with laughter bubbling out instead of fear in their voices. Marti rolled around the ground, played games and chase with the cousins while Victor played in the sand box he found in the back yard. Victor loved playing in the dirt with the trucks. By five o'clock he was filthy from head to toe, but smiling from ear to ear. Aunt Marie wanted the children to have baths before we set out for home. It was a two and a half hour drive; if they fell asleep they would be nice and clean when put to bed. I shook as fear instantly filled me. I tried to say no, Victor didn't need a bath; the bruises had to be kept hidden - no one could find out. Tim warned me I would lose my kids, because I let him beat them, I didn't keep them in line and it was my fault. She started the bath anyway filling the tub with nice warm water and lots of bubbles.

I said I would give my son his bath; I waited until she left, took off his clothes then into the tub he went and truly enjoyed it. The bruises were still very prominent on his little body, but now at least they didn't hurt. Some small consolation that was! I was drying Victor when Aunt Marie unexpectedly came in through the door and saw the bruises. She stood there with absolute shock on her face. She could not believe what she was seeing on this small innocent boy. What in the world happened to him? My voice cracking, I told her what Tim had done. How he shut me out of the room and took the belt to Victor. Filled with anger and rage, she went into the kitchen and laid into Tim for all to hear. Stating in a very threatening voice that Victor is a precious little boy and he better never touch him again or he would have her to deal with. Everyone stood around stunned by what they were hearing. Tim didn't say much. I'm sure he had some excuse, he always did. Needless to say, I got chastised for letting her see the bruises, but this time nothing else happened to my son. For once someone stood up to him, little good it did. Fat lips, more bruises, kicks, punches as well as mental abuse just to name a few of the things the children had to endure over the years. People don't know what goes on behind closed doors. I had to continue hiding the physical and mental abuse in order to keep my children from being taken away, always his threats hanging over my head.

As for Aunt Marie, we saw her many, many times after that and to my knowledge never once did she ask if the abuse was still occurring. So much denial so close to home.

5. *Judo*

Tim always had to have the upper hand in everything no matter what it was. So taking Judo was his new "upper hand." He started taking classes at the base one or two days a week.

Once Tim started taking these classes, he would come home and after supper he would show off his new moves. He would try them on the children first and surprisingly was pretty easy going. But with me, he wanted to show how the moves actually worked. I felt it was either the children, or I, so I got practiced on. Every time I would hit the floor hard or get an arm-twisted in some painful way. I told him he was being too rough, but he said I just didn't know the counter moves. *Bull*! When your arm is being twisted back or a leg pulled out from under you so you slam down to the floor every time it doesn't matter about counter moves. Counter moves don't matter especially when it is your husband doing the moves, hurting you and not seeing the pain and suffering which; he himself is inflicting. He only wants to show he is in command, he is in charge and he has complete power! In his mind he thought it would be helpful for us to learn self-defense. Marti was being picked on in school, as was Victor. We went to a class and the instructor showed us some basic moves to defend ourselves. Marti never used them and when Victor did, he paid dearly for it with severe consequences from his father.

Judo is supposed to teach self-control and discipline. Victor decided to show one of the kids at school some discipline for picking on him. He felt it was self defense, because he was always getting hit, called names, ambushed, and whatever else the kids could do to him to be cruel. On the way home from school he had enough from this one particular kid. He picked on Victor relentlessly. Victor turned around and kicked the kid hard enough in the stomach to double him over. The kid went home crying telling his parents that Victor kicked him for no apparent reason. His parents called the police. A short while after Tim got home, the police showed up at our front door. ***Oh my God what would happen to my son now?*** Fear struck me hard. I felt sick all over, and Victor's face told me that he knew with absolute certainty he was in for a beating of his life after the police left. Basically the policeman warned Victor not to kick the other boy again and said that the kids had to get along. He said that he understood that kids fight once in a while, but also let Victor know that charges could be pressed and, were that to happen, that Victor would be in big trouble. Little did the officer know that Victor was *already* in big trouble!

After the officer left, Tim went ballistic, screaming and hollering at Victor for embarrassing him and causing trouble. While pushing him around, Tim screamed at Victor, telling him that he only showed him that move for *extreme* situations. Then, I couldn't believe what had just happened - Tim turned around, kicked our son in the stomach, and asked how *he* liked it. Victor doubled over and fell to the floor. His father told him to get up. Once he did, Victor got hit again and knocked down hard again and yelled at over and over. Then, he was grounded on top of being grounded previously. I tried talking to Tim, telling him that Victor was always being picked on and that in his mind; it was an extreme measure and defended himself. Of course, Tim didn't want to hear anything I had to say. Victor had enough and wanted to show that he had the upper hand. I thought to myself, his father *taught* him well.

Tim always told Victor to watch out for the hand you don't see. That unseen hand would always punch Victor, except on this one particular day. Victor let his father have a high-quality punch right in the stomach. He slugged him hard with his own unseen hand. He then looked at his father with a smirk on his face and said, "Watch the hand you don't see dad". His father couldn't do a thing about it. It is what he had been doing to him for months. I was so glad when Tim was unable to sign the two of them up for classes together. I knew if they practiced together Victor would get hurt. After a while this phase of Tim's finally ended. It took about two years. He didn't have time anymore and now we didn't have to be the victims of his practices. But it didn't mean we still didn't get hit or batted around, especially Victor.

6. Still More Degrading Sex

Living two houses away from his folks, we could see each other from our back yards. I was out back one day standing on the pool deck. It was a beautiful day. I saw Tim over his folks; he had stopped by on his way home from work. I yelled over to him and said hi. He just glared at me. Dread filled me instinctively. I felt that something was terribly wrong. When he got home he was in a really bad mood, a quiet menacing bad. I didn't know why. What did I do this time? I had been at work all day, gotten the children, came home and started supper. I didn't have time for anything else and had no friends. While appearing calm, I was frantically trying to figure out what I had done wrong. We had a quiet supper that night, and then he sent the children to bed.

He wanted to talk to me. He told me that I was a whore and that he wanted me out, adding that he was not going to let his children live with a slut. Shocked and dumbfounded, I looked at him. I didn't know what the heck he was talking about. The way I felt about sex he should have known that there was no way in hell I would find sex elsewhere. I was without a car that day and was given a ride home from one of the girls at work. When he went to pick me up after work, which he said he wasn't going to do; I wasn't there. He was told I left with the guy I always ate lunch with. Right away he thought I was cheating on him. He gave me no benefit of the doubt, nothing-just accusations. I screamed at him telling him it wasn't true, but he kept calling me names and telling me I was lying. He called me a whore again so I slapped his face, which; didn't help the situation at all. That made him angrier and more threatening to me. I stood there shaking, crying and pleading with him to stop, to believe me; but he just kept calling me names and saying I was being deceitful. There was no reasoning with him as his mind was made up. He was the only one to have a say in this conversation, even if it meant the end of our marriage.

First of all, I never ate lunch with a guy; and secondly I always ate with a bunch of girls. We all sat together at one of the production lines.

I was devastated. The next day when I went to work, I went in and talked to my boss. I asked how someone could do that to me. He didn't know and felt bad for me. I started asking around to see if anyone knew anything or heard anything.

Then it came up, that yes Samantha did have lunch every day with a guy. But it was another Samantha. She ate lunch every day with her brother. When Tim asked about Samantha that person just assumed it was her and not me he was asking about. I went home that night and told Tim what happened. He just looked at me; I couldn't tell what he was thinking, but as always to make things better we had sex that night.

We never made love; it was always just sex. By this time whenever I was upset after sex or after another bad day of his put downs, I would curl up into a little ball on the farthest side of the bed nearest to the top and I would cry myself to sleep. I needed to be as far away from the pain and hurt as possible. I didn't want him to touch me and I didn't want to be near him in any way shape or form. Tim's demands for sex were continually getting worse and he wanted sex every night. I hated it more and more. I even looked forward to when Mother Nature would arrive. That was my only salvation. At least it was a week without sex, well most of the time. If Tim wanted sex while Mother Nature was around we would have to get in the shower. I would have to bend over and he would go at it with my head hitting the wall with each thrust. The shower was small and as hard as I tried, I couldn't keep myself from hitting the wall. Of course complaining about it didn't help. Sometimes I just couldn't get out of having sex. After he was finished I would have to go into the bathroom and search for the tampon that he shoved way up inside of me because of his selfish needs. I would then take a shower to try and cleanse the filth away. Now he was introducing dirty books and movies into our sex sessions. His end table was filled with porn books, girly magazines, sex videos and lubricant. He even bought a dildo.

We would go to the video store on Friday nights to pick out family movies. The children and I would go into the Disney or comedy section to find something funny, or happy. Tim always went straight to the x-rated section. I was always so embarrassed and immediately tensed up. I knew what was in store for me that night. He would put on a good act, I would make popcorn and we would sit down and watch a movie with the children. Then, after I put them to bed he would force me to take a shower. I would take forever, I knew what was coming and I despised it and him. Then into the bedroom we went. He had already warned the children not to come in. If they needed us, they had better knock on the door first. He would go into the basket of slinky nighties and pick something out for me to put on. I hated that basket so much I kept it hidden in the back upper most corner of my closet, but he knew where it was. Once he turned on the video, he would get behind me and he would take out the lubricant and put large amounts of it on his penis. He only used the dildo a few times, thank God. I was forced to watch the movie, but I always closed my eyes. They were disgusting and degrading to me. He would then rub his penis against my rectum for at least 30 minutes or more and then insert the head, penetrating me from behind. I hated him more and more for that. I begged him not to have sex that way, but he only wanted what he wanted. Sometimes he would push harder and farther in and I would end up crying and pleading with him to stop. But he would not stop until he was ready. The same would go on with the dirty books. I would just flip pages making believe I was reading them, all the time hating him. Sometimes he would just turn me over, finish himself and start yelling at me. I kept trying to tell him how much it hurt, that it was not what I wanted, it was uncomfortable and he was too big. As I stood there looking into his angry eyes he would put me down. His response was always the same; he said I was lying, how bad at sex I was and how frigid I was.

Many times he wanted oral sex. That, for me was even more degrading than the rest. I felt it was dirty. I didn't want to do that. For me it was not right. Tim had all the answers. If two people love each other they should want to explore everything. Yes, but in my opinion, if both people agree and feel right doing it. I certainly did not agree and I certainly did not love him. The kind of sex I had with Tim, for the most of our marriage, was non consensual. All through our marriage I had to come up with ways to survive for the children and myself and this was just another way of surviving. I would make sure the lights were out and rub his penis on the outside of my cheek and move my tongue around hoping he was so into *his sex* that I would get away with it. It worked for a while and then he mentioned that he knew what I was doing. Instant panic set in. I knew I was going to be forced to do what he wanted and couldn't get out of it. The condoms came home, so I wouldn't have to taste him. How nice of him. He just wanted his sex. My feelings just didn't matter in the least little bit to him. Still I refused to do it. I would gag and want to throw up and sometimes I did. After our degrading sex session I would go into the bathroom and scour my mouth out with mouthwash, toothpaste and constantly rinse to get the awfulness of what just happened out of my mouth. Thank God; he never had an orgasm in my mouth.

We had many fights over this subject. He just didn't care how I felt and couldn't see past what his own needs were. He would even record the videos he rented. The movies didn't have a plot to them just plain sex, oral, anal and what every way was thought up on the video. Group sex was involved in the movies and the more girls in it the better he liked it.

The children had to either stay outside or in their rooms all day while he would record two or three of those nasty movies. They knew their father was taping dirty movies. How dare he subject our beautiful children to such filth at such an early age? Some days I would barely walk in the house or I would be doing dishes or some chore and he would call me and be at the bedroom door with his penis in his hand waving it at me. I was disgusted just looking at him, my stomach would turn upside down immediately at the thought of him touching me. If I couldn't get out of it, I would fake having an orgasm just to get it over with. Later sometimes after sex, I couldn't go back into the bedroom, because he would be in there masturbating again. He was never satisfied and never had enough sex. He was obsessed with it and sex meant more to him than his children or me.

When he had been drinking, it would take him forever to orgasm, half-hour to 45 minutes of him pounding away at me because of the alcohol. The only thing good about it was that he only wanted straight sex when he'd been drinking; I didn't have to worry about anal or oral sex, or whatever else he might have had in store for me.

By the time we got divorced 19 years later we only had sex on the weekends. I was working third shift so we were not on the same schedule. Of course he complained all the time about being weekend lovers. I was so glad - only two days a week now – but, of course, the same stuff was always involved. I still had to fear him coming in and waking me up for non consensual sex. He would just get into bed and have sex with me. I had to work all night but that didn't matter as long as he got what he wanted. I could only dream of what a real loving sexual relationship would be like.

7. Scouts and Camping

When we first got married we went camping a few times with my brother Harry and Moe. I didn't enjoy camping much because we only had a tent. It was a lot of work, and the children were little. If it rained there was no place to get dry. I remember one time we went camping with my brother and we were all outside the tent talking. Victor was in the tent playing. He was really into batman then; he had a batman on a string and was swinging it around playing and laughing having a good time. There was a crash, something got broken. There was anger written all over Tim's face as he stormed into the tent, the next thing we saw was my son literally come flying out of the tent, hit the picnic table and fall to the ground. Tim was so mad at him, because he broke the lantern. His father's actions were not justified. Victor was just playing and hit the lantern by mistake. He was moving a sleeping bag it brushed up against the lantern and knocked it over. Tim kept yelling at him. He was so irrational not letting Victor say anything in response. My brother couldn't believe what just happened. The astonishment and shock that Tim would do something like that to his own son was inconceivable to him. He took Tim aside and told him that what he had just done was child abuse. He certainly could have hurt Victor worse than he did. Harry also told him that if anyone had witnessed him doing such a thing they could call the police and have him arrested. Tim did not heed my brother's words because the abuse continued. No one could penetrate his irrationality. We were doomed to lives of fear and intimidation. I told Tim I wouldn't go camping anymore, I didn't like it and we could never get dry when it rained. A few years later he bought a little 15-foot Star camper. It was okay, but very small for two adults and two children. Once the children got a little bigger, he decided to get a pop up camper, which was much better. We had room to move around and a place to go when it rained. It was always up to me to make sure everything was packed and ready to go. On the road trip to the campground he said I had to be his eyes on the passenger side. He said he couldn't see and I had to keep a look out for him, so he could move in and out of traffic. It was very stressful, I would have to call out "clear" for him to move over and "no" for him to stay put. It was hard to judge sometimes with a trailer behind and I misjudged a few times. When I did, he really tore into me for it. He would say that I was trying to get us all killed and that I should be able to judge by now, I'd been doing it long enough. Sometimes, if he couldn't see out the mirror on my side of the vehicle; without warning, his hand would lash out onto my forehead and slam my head back into the seat. Then he would scream at me to stay the hell out of his way. It was never a fun trip, singing songs, talking about the fun we would have. That was only a dream too.

We went camping with our neighbors one holiday weekend. Since Tim had to work, we got a late start. When we got to the campground it was dark and the pouring rain was soaking us to the bone. Tim was in a foul mood because of the conditions in which we had to set up. He was yelling at us constantly to do this or that and help out. Nothing we did was right in his mind. Someone finally took pity on us and came over to help set up after hearing him constantly berating us. For years we went camping and the same things happened repeatedly. He would put the camper in the garage on Monday and tell me to have it packed and ready to go by Friday when he got home from work. There was always so much tension packing, setting up and unpacking and then of course coming home and cleaning up every time we'd gone camping. He would not pack his own clothes, I had to pack for all of us and I would really get screamed at if something of his was forgotten. At first it was okay, but progressively he put more and more responsibility on me. He would help set up the camper and then take off with his buddies or sit and read. The inside of the camper was up to me to set up as were meals. All things, clothes, food, sleeping bags and anything we brought with us had to be neat and orderly in the camper at all times, if it wasn't he would have a tantrum and we would pay for it. It was not fun or enjoyable for anyone but Tim. Once in a while he cooked on the open fire, but I had to have everything ready for him, and he would never help clean up afterward. We started camping a lot with my sister and brother when our children were older. They each had a canoe, so that meant we had to have one to go canoeing with them. Moe stored his canoe in our garage and said we could use it anytime we wanted. I hated it, it was too heavy, and the children and I had to help lower it from the ceiling, put it on the camper and tie it down. A few times we dropped the canoe and got yelled at for it. Even if the canoe fell and hit one of us in the shoulder or head, and that certainly hurt, he would just tell us we were inept and tell us to keep going. He just didn't get that the thing was way too heavy for the three of us to lift. Once at the campground, we had to take down the canoe and if we went to the lake we had to help carry it down to the waterfront. The canoeing itself was fun but the preparation for it was nerve racking and always had us tense.

When Tim had guard duty on a camping weekend, he would leave and come back later and I had better have things closed up and ready to go. One time the children and I drove to the campground ourselves, he was going to meet us there. I was so nervous; first of all I never drove the wagon with the camper hitched to it and secondly I knew how particular he was about having everything set up perfectly. We got to the site and started to set up, all I did was yell at the children. My daughter just looked at me with frustration, fear and sadness in her eyes. I was like her father yelling at them constantly. Even the other campers were staring at me. I felt like a fool. I didn't want to be like him, but he had me on edge all the time. I knew I had to have the camper set up and arranged perfectly, to his specs, before he arrived. As the sweat ran down my back and my hands shook we continued and finally got the camper set up and did a decent job of it. What a relief he didn't complain when he got to the site, *but I have always regretted that for that moment I turned into someone I didn't like.*

A large group of families went camping on Labor Day weekend. It always rained that weekend and this weekend was no different. Pleasantly enough the first two nights were okay. It was nice out, however; the rain was due to start during our last night. I suggested that we pack up and leave early before the rain started, hoping in that way everything would be dry. If the camper got packed during the rain everything had to be dried out. It took days to dry especially if it continued to rain during the following week. We were packing the camper; I was inside because something got jammed in the rails and the bed would not slide in. Tim got mad and while I was on the bed he gave it a tremendous shove. I literally flipped over and landed on my shoulder on the floor of the camper. Everyone was watching and couldn't believe he had just done that. Someone asked if I was all right. I told them yes, but I was aching because my shoulder hurt and humiliated because of what they had seen, so I just kept packing. On another trip we ventured to New Hampshire and took his father's boat. Tim had always wanted the boat so his father let us borrow it for the weekend. The launch was not close to where we were camping so the children and I were made to drag the boat through the mucky water and weeds to the dock so we could go for a ride. I recall my daughter getting truly scared. "Mommy the water is too deep, I can't reach the bottom." I told her to hold on tight to the rope and she would be okay." I stayed close to her, she was so frightened and neither of us knew how to swim. Victor was in the boat as he was really too little to try and help; **heck** for that matter, so was my daughter. Tim's father had the boat for many years. Now, because we borrowed the boat we had to start taking two vehicles camping. I drove the wagon with the camper behind it and Tim drove the truck with the boat behind it. We didn't have a choice; we had to go out on the boat every day. Tim always decided what we would do and when we would do it. We had no say. Sometimes he would leave the children on the beach; he would then drive to a little cove where he had to have sex with me. Unbelievable right there on the floor of the boat or up on the banks behind some tree. I was terrified to get caught and it was rough either way. The floor of the boat was hard, cold and wet and there was no room to move. The ground on the banks was muddy, dirty, prickly and full of bugs. I hated it. Tim of course thought it was exciting, but it sure as hell wasn't for me. Not only was it uncomfortable, but my children were on the beach alone and unattended. Other than his sex and boating, we didn't do much together camping. If it were vacation he would just read or go out on the boat for hours. I had to make sure lunch was prepared and that we had snacks and plenty to drink. The children did enjoy jumping into the water off the boat and they did enjoy being pulled on a tube. As for myself, I learned how to water-ski. But lots of times the children and I would do our own thing and that, in my memory, were the best times. Marti and I went for a hike one day. We were gone for hours. We hiked to the top of a mountain, the view was fantastic and we had a great time. We chatted about the trees, the animals we saw and just being out there where it was so peaceful and out of harm's way. Little did we know how much trouble we would be in when we got back? Tim couldn't find us. I *told* him we were going for a hike - even asked him to go with us, but he didn't listen as usual. But, to Marti and me, it was worth getting yelled at because we got to enjoy each other's company without the usual tension that enveloped us. We got to enjoy the splendor of all we had seen.

Tim's aunt and uncle were to celebrate their 25th wedding anniversary. A large celebration was planned for them in Vermont. We were invited and made the necessary arrangements to attend. Tim wanted to make a big weekend of it and decided we would go camping. We set up the camper that night and the next day we decided to go down to the beach for a swim. He took off his watch and told me to hold it. I put it on the chair while we were in the water with the children. When it was time to go back to the camper it slipped my mind that the watch was still on the chair. When we got to the camper he asked for his watch. I did not have it. It had fallen off the chair when everything was packed up. He was being irrational. "I told you to hold my watch. I am so sick and tired of you being incapable of doing anything I tell you to do." He was berating me, putting me down and screaming at me in front of the children. Again, he was humiliating me. I tried to explain to him that it was on the chair, but he refused to listen to anything I said and just kept putting me down. Then he told me he was so tired of all the bullshit and of me being so inadequate that he wanted a divorce. Everyone going by could hear his disgusting mouth. Thinking back, that should have been a happy moment for me. I should have taken him up on wanting a divorce, but of course in my frame of mind and the poor image I had of myself it was inconceivable. He had belittled me for so long, I felt I was a failure at everything and could never make it on my own. My son and I went out of the camper and started to walk to the office to see if anyone had turned in the watch. I was so upset and feeling like such a loser that I collapsed. My son started yelling, "Mom, are you okay?" Tim even asked if I was okay, which surprised me, but he didn't bother to help me. I just looked at him and said," What do you care?" I got up unsteady and unsure of anything and walked with my son the half-mile to the office to see about that damn watch. When we got back it was late, we didn't speak a word to each other and went to bed. The next day we got up and got ready for the party. Tim ignored me all the way there and at the party. The entire time he would not look at me nor would he dance with me. He would not even acknowledge I was there. Someone in his family asked if I was okay. They could see I was upset and I'm sure could feel the tension between us. I said we had an argument and that things were fine. Someone had turned in his watch before we left. The next day we packed up and went home where he again told me how useless I was. He told me how his walls were closing in on him and that he was feeling smothered. "Things better change or I am out of here and you will lose everything. If you don't want to lose the children you better straighten up." That was my warning notice, a*gain*.

Along with camping was scouting. Tim had been into scouts all his life and had gotten back into it after he met some guys at the Elks club. He was gone quite a lot, three or four nights a week, which the children and I didn't mind. It was peaceful with him gone. We didn't have to worry about his temper going off; he would be occupied with other things.

Now that Victor was of age, Tim said he had to be in the scouts. Victor never asked about scouting, but he would join the troop just to please his father. It was a way to spend time with him, even if it was in the same room with 20 other boys.

This is what Tim got Victor into, but I had to make sure Victor went to his meetings. It was up to me to drop him off, pick him up and make snacks if it was his turn to bring them. I had to get up early on weekends, make sure he was packed for overnight camping trips and bring him to the drop off point. Tim was too busy being a big shot scout leader. We had to go to dances, fundraisers, camping trips and many more events that Tim wanted us to be involved in. What Tim wanted is what Tim got over and over again. He wanted to look good, look like he took good care of us.

Tim signed the two of them up for scout camp every year. I was told about Victor complaining one day because he didn't feel well. He didn't want to go for the Polar swim. The boys had to get up at six in the morning and go swimming before breakfast. Victor was sick and didn't want to go. He said his stomach hurt. But his father made him go just the same. Jimmy told me later that Victor threw up in the tent once they got back from the swim and that he was terribly sick all day. Tim wanted Victor to make Eagle Scout. That is what Tim wanted, not what Victor wanted. Victor could care less. He just wanted time with his father. Victor kept going to scouts every year and changing troops, because his father was never satisfied with the one he was in. Victor never made Eagle Scout. He stopped going to scouts when his father and I separated. He just didn't care. His Eagle project was done and all Victor needed to make Eagle

Scout was two badges. It was never scouting he was after; he was looking for a way to gain his father's love, approval and attention. It didn't work and it broke my heart to watch.

The Explorers are what Marti joined. She really enjoyed it. They went caving a lot and she made many friends. Tim was glad that she was in a scout program. They went camping at Camp Hyapoe. Tim went there a lot when he was little so that is all we heard about. A winter camping trip was planned at Camp Hyapoe on this one weekend. Troops from all over the state would be attending the camp-out. Tim had a big hand in planning this outing. Marti was really excited to go and she wanted all of us to be there with her. She was in a senior troop and they would be doing the cooking and organizing activities. It was in the middle of the winter and it was bitter cold out. Tim knew I didn't like the cold. I got cold very easy and it took me forever to warm up. Luck was with me this day. I was able to stay indoors and keep the fireplace going for the scouts when they came in to eat and get warm. I loved it. The fireplace was huge and had lots of wood to burn. That is how I spent my day stoking the fire adding more wood and keeping it blazing hot so everyone could warm up when they came inside.

8. *Jekyll and Hyde*

It baffled me, everywhere we went and everyone we met loved Tim. They thought he was such a good leader at scouts or in college, but they didn't know the other side of him; the side that was like a toggle that would switch on and off so quickly. Like Jekyll and Hyde, we never knew what was coming or when it would happen, but he always appeared level headed with everyone else. He had to please them and be the best in each person's eyes. Everyone else came first and Tim let us know it. We were going over my mom's for dinner one Sunday evening. Tim was in a really bad mood. As usual things were not to his liking and it set him off again. The children and I got screamed at, at home and in the car all the way over to my mom's. "Why can't you ever have things the way they are supposed to be"? "Why can't you have the house clean?' "Why can't you kids do as you are told?" "Why can't you kids clean your rooms?" "Why don't you do as I say?" Tim's way, always his way. He was unrelenting when it came to what he wanted and how he wanted things to be. He was unwilling to compromise or to see another person's point of view. We were never good enough. It had to be done his way. When we got there Tim warned the children to behave or they would have hell to pay when we got home. The minute the car door was opened he was a changed person bad guy out good guy in! All smiles, happy face and loving all around. Yet, family members in the house could sense the tension between us. They knew what was going on but couldn't do much about it. In addition, if they said anything it would make matters worse and we all knew it. Most of the time, regardless of what happened, I would say it was my fault and conceal the rest of what was happening to us. The minute we got in the car to go home, Hyde was back. He started bellowing at us all over again, all the way home and into the house repeating how bad we were and how inadequate we were. Once he finished putting us all down for the umpteenth time, he would send the children to bed and we would go into the dreaded bedroom for another one of his demeaning sex sessions.

Tim had hurt his back at work and was in a lot of pain. We were going over to his sister's for a party and I had to drive. Tim usually drove, another way to control me. All the way over he yelled at me to stop hitting bumps and stop driving so fast. I was driving 30 miles an hour and making sure I was being careful, but he didn't want to see it. Again, when we got out of the car he changed. He let people know how much pain he was in, but he stopped yelling at me right away. On the way home the same thing again, Hyde was back again, be careful stop going so fast my back hurts. "Why can't you be a better driver? You know I'm in pain why can't you be more careful?" So now on top of all my other faults, I was a terrible driver too. There was little left that I could do right and I foolishly believed him.

Time and again, people would come over or we would go out, he would flip his switch and be a different person. The person he wanted people to see and like would come out, but when they left, the true Tim came back. The dark side, the menacing side was back and we suffered dearly. The children would get yelled at, Victor would get smacked, Marti would get poked in the chest, and they would get grounded and sent to their rooms. I would get yelled at and put down, "Can't you keep this house clean, and can't you control the kids, why can't you be better and do as you are supposed to?" But then, he would expect me to have sex with him. But I didn't have a switch. He did. Tim would then demand his dirty sex and would hurt me. It was not consensual. He would not listen to me when I said it hurt or disagreed with what he wanted. I would cry a lot, but hid it from him time and time again because it only infuriated him all the more. I would be berated even more and he would get angrier with me. Then he would give me either the cold shoulder for a few days or he would just give me a mean and nasty attitude. But, always, no matter how he felt about me he would want his sex. It was always his obsession and priority. He destroyed things when he got mad.

When Victor was a small boy, he was a little clumsy at times. But I didn't think anything of it - little boys are awkward when in a growth spurt. However, Victor broke something of Tim's one day and his father got unbelievably mad at him. I don't remember what the item was that got broken though I do remember it being insignificant and of little value. Victor had gotten a new helicopter for his birthday. He absolutely loved it and played with it constantly. Tim went into his room, grabbed the helicopter, threw it on the floor, and stomped on it smashing it to pieces. Then he said to Victor," How do you like getting your things broken?" My little boy was crushed, he stood there with tears in his eyes, and his helicopter gone; smashed to bits by the hand of his father. He was only a little kid; he didn't mean to break things. How could Tim warrant his own behavior? This man, an adult chronologically, who had a son to love, cherish, protect and nurture, just broke his boy's favorite possession and his heart once again. Sure he made a point that he was in charge and had all the power, but at the expense of his child.

The children and I had gotten nothing done one particular day. We were playing with Lego bricks making a paper and pencil holder to put by the phone. We lost track of time working on this little project together. It came out great and the children and I had fun doing it. When Tim saw it after arriving home from work, he got angry and upset that we wasted so much of our time playing with toys. They had created something they were proud of, but it went unnoticed. Tim believed I couldn't spend quality time with my children unless it was on his terms. Hyde was out in full force and was certainly being ugly, so I did something I should not have done. I talked back to him and threw my keys at him. They didn't hit him, but landed on the floor near him, I knew if they hit him, he would, if truth were told, kill me. I don't know why I threw the keys, because I knew I would be in for it. He went *ballistic*, he threw the keys back at me then he took the paper and pencil holder we made and threw it across the room shattering it. Because I told him that it was not necessary for him to do that, he took his arm swiped it across the counter top taking everything with it knocking it all to the floor. As he came towards me telling me I had better not ever do anything like that again, I saw only rage in him. His face was red, lips tight together and pointed finger barreled down on me. I told the children to get lost. I wanted them out of their father's sight so they would not feel his fury, because of something I did. He was roaring mad, irrational; there was no talking to him. He pointed his finger in my face and warned me that under no circumstances was I ever to pull a stunt like that again. As he walked away he stated in an unemotional manner how the entire incident was my fault for not bowing down to him once again. Now in tears and shaking, I cleaned up another disaster that I know he undeniably created.

We had a lot of family picnics in Vermont. Most of his family lived there so we often went to visit or for a party. On this day we left the party around seven o'clock to drive home. We had only been to his aunt's new house a few times so Tim was going to follow his father. When we got to the top of the street, his father was able to merge into traffic without a problem. Tim however could not. There was a large line of cars coming down the road making it impossible for Tim to merge into the street traffic directly after his father. All of a sudden, so unexpectedly he took off like a bat out of hell. He slammed his foot to the gas pedal and took off, the car motor sounding like the roar of a jet engine about to take off. Tim was so angry and didn't care that he had eight people in the car. I could see the anger building in him. His face got beat red and his lips tensed right up. He caught up to his father and then passed him doing 90 miles an hour. I kept begging him to slow down and held onto the dash for dear life. His sister was screaming at him and had her fingers gripped into the back of his neck trying to get him to slow down. He didn't hear either his sister or me, or he chose not to hear, because he didn't slow down. When we finally pulled off at a rest stop, we all got out of the car and began to breathe again. But boy did his sister and their father lay into him. They both told him how foolish and reckless he was and how dare he take that many people's lives and put them in such danger. They told him he was irresponsible and irrational and that he better learn to curb his temper. His sister told him that if she had another way to get home, she would in no way get back into the car with him. He drove more carefully the rest of the way home, but I knew he was furious because someone had put him in his place. I could still sense it. I knew his moods and he was fuming inside and I knew that someone was going to pay for it. I told the children to go straight to bed when we got home, so they would not feel the impact of his outrage. They got off safe this time. I, however, got reprimanded and told never to tell him how to drive again, to mind my own freaking business and shut my mouth.

Tim could speed in the car but Marti could not park in the wrong spot at the mall or she would get grounded. She got a part time job at the mall and would drive to work. Tim insisted that she park in the back lot of the mall. He felt it was a safer place to park and it was another way to control her. He decided to check on her one day, she had parked in the front lot. Of course she got the car taken away from her. She had to walk to work. He didn't care what kind of weather it was. She would come home soaked from head to toe dripping wet because he refused to let me pick her up in a rainstorm. I don't mean a drizzle it would be a downpour. Like me, Marti was trying to defy her father in some small way. Also like me nothing ever worked to her advantage. On another occasion, after she was given back the privilege to use the car, she once again parked in the front lot. She called me crying; she was hysterical and knew she was in major trouble. She hit a car backing out of her spot. I went to the square and we called the police. There was absolutely no damage to our car, but she severely damaged the side of a brand new Aurora. The entire back door was creased from front to back. Someone had told Marti to leave and no one would know she hit the car. Marti knew better she stayed and did the right thing. I was so proud of her that day. The woman whose car she damaged was very nice about the situation and appreciated that we waited for her to come out. She even told Marti how responsible she thought she was for taking accountability for her actions. Now the wait was on. Terrible dread filled us both as we waited for Tim to get home. We knew with certainty that Marti was in deep trouble. The iron fist would come down with all its fury. Not only did Marti get screamed at, berated and put down. She was also told what a dumb thing she did and how irresponsible she was. And of course she now lost the privilege to use the car indefinitely. It had started to get cold out and the walks home for Marti were terribly cold. On this particular night the wind was blowing and it was bitter cold. Tim was in a half way descent mood for a change, so I decided to ask if I could pick up Marti at work. Immediately he changed. The rage, the fury the unwavering control was evident. I knew the answer without hearing it. NO! I begged him to let me pick her up. I was worried, not only was it bitter cold out but it was after 10 o'clock at night and about a mile's walk home. Tim refused, saying it would teach her a lesson. All it did was make her angrier and horribly sick. A short while later Marti walked into the house shaking, red and seriously pissed off and upset. Her face and hands were red and felt frozen. She had a look of total hatred and despise on her face as she walked into her room without a word to anyone.

We had gone camping and again we had his father's boat. Tim was pulling Victor in the tube when it flipped over. Victor hit a wave hard, sending him flying into the air about ten feet straight up, then smashing him down into the water hard, face first. I screamed, "Stop, stop, he's out!" My son was not moving, and he appeared to be knocked out. Tim immediately turned the boat around to get to our son. When we got to him he was waiting for us, a little shaken, but seemed fine. We pulled him into the boat and checked him out to make sure he was okay. Victor had enough tubing for the day. He didn't want to ride any more. He was scared and hurting from the impact of the water. Of course that was his father's clue to start in on him. One minute concerned that he was unconscious and the next he was yelling at him telling him he was a "wimp" and a "chicken shit." It was only one spill you need to get right back out there again. But Victor did not want to so the rest of the weekend his father berated him and called him a wimp every time we went on the boat. Not a fun weekend for us, but one of many. Part of Tim's Jekyll and Hyde persona is the fact that he truly did care for us in his own twisted way. It was the 4th of July, we were doing sparklers, and it was a windy day. Tim had his arms around Victor holding his hands with the sparkler, he was only two years old and wasn't old enough to hold it by himself. The wind blew the ash off the sparkler; it burned thru Victor's rubber pants and went into his diaper. It burned the side of his penis. I looked at Tim; he grabbed the hose and sprayed water into Victor's diaper to stop the burning. I wrapped him in a towel and we brought him to the emergency room. They just about accused us of child abuse. (Little did they know what was truly going on in our house of horror)? Hysterically, the nurse was told the diaper was in the car if she wanted to see it. Then the doctor came in and said he had seen some strange things happen and that he believed me.

Another time, it was Christmas Eve. I was to stay home with the children while Tim went to midnight mass with his family. Victor was very sick. He was wheezing, running a fever and was incredibly pale. I called right before they left for mass, and told Tim that Victor was not breathing properly. Tim and his father rushed right over. We took Victor to the emergency room where he was treated for bronchitis. In the morning we let Victor sleep as he had a terrible night. We were all exhausted from the night before and decided to take our time with the morning events. Tim's sister called and asked where we were. He told her we would be there when we got there. They should realize that Victor needed extra time that morning because he had been so sick the night before. That went over like a lead balloon. Minutes later his parents came over and screamed at us for putting a damper on the holiday. How dare we hold up the usual Christmas tradition? Tim stuck up for us that morning. He told his parents that they should know how sick Victor was during the night because his father was with us and he had also told his sister we would be there a little later.

On this Christmas Eve, Victor was again sick. Because of his asthma, he was having a hard time breathing. His Peak Flow Meter (breathing monitor) indicated that he was in the red zone, which was not a good sign. This meant he was only getting 50% or less of the amount of oxygen required to breathe properly. I called the doctor's office because he was wheezing and extremely pale. The answering service said they would get hold of the doctor right away. The doctor was at a party. I was called a few minutes later and told to get Victor to the doctor's office immediately.

Victor and I were at the office about three hours. The doctor gave him a number of treatments for his asthma. He was only breathing at 50% (the red zone) when we arrived; when we left he was up to 80% (the high yellow zone). The doctor said he was bad enough for the hospital, but he would rather not put Victor in on Christmas Eve. When we got home Tim started screaming at me for being gone so long without calling him. He knew we were at the doctor's office, he should have gone with us, but he didn't feel like it. The doctor had me bring Victor to the office every day for the next four days to monitor his breathing and give him treatments with the nebulizer (breathing machine). He wanted to make sure his breathing was stabilized so he would not be put into the hospital during the holidays. Victor hadn't been feeling well; his asthma was acting up again. When he said he was going to be sick I told him to go to the bathroom. He didn't make it. He got sick all over the floor and all over the dog. I could not clean it up as it was making me sick. Wow, to my complete astonishment Tim cleaned everything up for me. He had Victor take a bath; he washed the dog and even washed the kitchen floor for me.

Victor flipped over the handlebars on his bike one day and really scraped up his face. The skin was gone from his nose and his lips were swollen and bruised. Tim took him right to the doctor to get checked out. He was okay but for days his sweet little face was so scraped up and swollen.

Marti had to have her tonsils out, Tim was right there by my side while we waited. Marti had to have six teeth pulled. Both times her beautiful face looked as if someone stuck a basketball in it. Tim was there;

again, always showing that he did care when they were sick or hurting. However was oblivious or didn't care how much hurt he himself inflicted onto them, whether physical or emotional.

Tim sent the children outside to clean the yard on this particular day. It was another one of their chores. He yelled at them telling them they better do a good job or they would be doing it over. They were out back by the fence cleaning the leaves away from it. There were some old car parts leaning against the fence. Tim had a cement block on top of a pipe to keep the water out of it. Victor leaned against the fence not knowing it would spring back and send the cement block off the pipe. The block fell and hit Marti's foot. By the time she came into the house, which only took a minute she had a huge goose egg on the top of her foot. Tim called his father and we went to the emergency room. Tim was there again. Thank goodness nothing was broken but she did have a bad bruise, a huge black and blue egg on her foot and had to use crutches for a few days.

But don't let this fool you. Keep in mind Tim could change in a heartbeat and lots of times he did. As for me, when I was hurt, he showed little concern and if I was sick he let me know it by constantly complaining or making a big fuss about having to fix supper, so that I would finally get up and do it.

A few times I was really sick so he would get his parents to take care of the children for him. One time he had no choice I almost passed out and could not stand up without being dizzy. I had bronchitis to the point it was almost pneumonia, my ears were completely blocked and my head was severely stuffed. He put me to bed and I do remember him checking on me a number of times.

Another time I had to call him home from work. I had severe pains in my chest and in my stomach. When he got home I could barely move there was such pain. He brought me right to the emergency center and even carried me in. The doctor said it was muscle spasms in my back, but it turned out to be a gall bladder attack.

While working in a factory, I developed carpal tunnel in both my wrists. It was very painful. My hands would go numb at night and I would wake up crying because they hurt so badly. I would be on the phone or have a glass of water in my hand, my hand would go numb and I would drop whatever was in it. Finally, I had to have surgery on my left hand - it was the worst of the two. About ten years later and after starting my home day care, I had to have surgery on my right hand. I explained the circumstances to all the parents and they had no problem coming in and setting up what was needed for their child in the morning. It was decided the surgery would be done on a Friday, so I could have the weekend to rest. I knew from past experience the first few days would be the worst. Tim was really nice that day. He stayed by my side the whole time and after the surgery he took me to lunch. I still felt no pain and felt fairly good, but couldn't cut my food. Being right handed and having it wrapped up made it quite difficult for me, he cut my food and helped me out all day. That night he made sure my medication was taken and put me to bed. But like Jekyll and Hyde, the next night was totally different. We were invited to a party for his niece. I wasn't doing well. The pain was awful and the medication was making me sick. I was getting dizzy and felt like I was going to vomit. I wanted to stay home, but he absolutely refused to let me. He stated that it was a function for his godchild's birthday and we all needed to go as a family. I sat on the couch at the party in tears, my hand swollen, throbbing and constantly in pain. To keep from vomiting I had to take deep breaths. When his mother came in she didn't say a thing to me, she didn't want to upset me further. She knew I should have been home in bed, but again didn't want to mention anything to Tim for fear of the wrath he would wreak upon us again. Tim's uncle knew how he was because he had seen Tim's temper in action. He took me upstairs and let me lie on his bed. After steadying my head from the dizziness, I finally went to sleep. Tim came up later to get me and was being miserable and irrational. He told me it would have been nice for me to stay down stairs and how dare I go lay down and embarrass him. All the way home he belittled me and yelled at me for being insensitive to his needs. When we got home I went into the bedroom to get ready for bed, I felt dreadful and had cried all the way home. I felt sick, dizzy and was in severe pain. As I was getting undressed he started on the children. I don't know what they did. It was quite possible and more than likely that he was irritated with me for embarrassing him at the party and he had to take it out on someone else and unfortunately it was the children. I didn't know what was going on. All of a sudden everything was going black. I could not breathe; my head was swimming and felt like I was going to be sick. I remember falling to the floor; the only thing in my head as I fell to the floor was his voice repeatedly yelling at the children. He was so busy hollering at them that he didn't know I had fainted. When I came to, he was still hollering at them. After he finished berating the children he sent them to their rooms.

I wasn't able to call his name because of the weakness that over took me. He didn't know how hard it was for me to pull myself up, because he was too busy bullying the children.

I crawled into bed once the children were in their rooms. I knew then they would be okay. As sick as I was I was still aware of the constant threat and turmoil the children had to endure. I don't remember any more that night.

The next few weeks were hard. I still had to work, in my home day care and that meant that the parents brought their children no matter what. Never a day off! It took me a long time to do things and of course Tim would be upset, because things were not done or set when he said they should be. The children had to help me more because of his demanding ways. He would come home and still expect supper prepared and the house clean. His way of helping was to call and order a pizza. Big deal!

Victor was a thumb sucker starting at four months old. He liked to put his fingers in the tag of his stuffed animals and rub them together while sucking his thumb. We tried lots of things to get him to stop but nothing worked. When he was about four all the tags were cut off his stuffed animals. I thought if he didn't have the tags it would help him stop. I then tried nail-biter polish, it taste terrible. That didn't work and neither did putting pepper on his thumb. After a year of trying to get him to stop I figured he would stop when he needed to. It wasn't a real concern for me. He was a kid and would stop sucking his thumb when ready, but his father said that wasn't good enough and that he was too old to be sucking his thumb. What Tim said was law. That is when his father started to bite Victor's thumb. The first time Tim bit Victor's thumb he was sitting on Victor's bed talking to him. He took hold of his hand and bit down on that little thumb extremely hard. He then told Victor that is what he would get every time he would catch him sucking his thumb. I can still picture the deep impressions of his teeth in Victor's small thumb. Victor would cry and not be able to move his thumb for hours, but he still didn't stop sucking it. Because he wouldn't stop, Tim started to smack him as well as continue to bite Victor's thumb. This was one of the few times I stood up to him but not without paying the consequences for days after. I *demanded* that he stop chomping on Victor's thumb. I pushed that little boy's thumb in his father's face and showed him what he had done. He had bitten it so many times, and so brutally, that the thumb was swollen and infected. It was green and yellow in color, with red around the edges.

I tried to get Victor to keep the thumb out of his mouth, especially now that it was infected but he just wouldn't stop. Every time he would hear his father approaching he would dry off his thumb and hide it. He knew the pain that would be inflicted upon him if he were caught sucking it. He needed something to comfort himself, his father never did. At about eight years old Victor finally did stop sucking his thumb.

Victor started to wet the bed because of his insecurities and fears. I would give him little to drink after supper so he would not have an accident. I'd also get him up in the middle of the night and have him go to the bathroom. Tim was always gone when the children got up in the morning. I would wash and dry the bedclothes and remake the bed before Tim got home from work. Victor wouldn't get into trouble too often for wetting his bed, because we hid it most of the time. I would have liked a husband who would have helped solve the problem with me: one who would have cared enough to help Victor overcome his insecurities and bed-wetting.

Because of the frustration Victor felt, he would be very angry all the time. Victor had a nasty temper and would often take things out on the house. One occasion he kicked the wall in his bedroom and put his foot through it. There was a huge gaping hole in the wall by his closet door. Dread filled both of us immediately. We knew he would once again get beaten and put down when his father found out what he had done, even though he had actually learned this behavior from Tim.

Victor decided to move his room around to hide the hole. It lasted for a few days until his father decided to go into his room shoving things around complaining it was nothing but a big pig sty. He called Victor to his room and I knew what was about to happen. I followed behind Victor. I knew he was in deep trouble. We both stood looking at the hole in the wall. Tim looked at me with rage because we had hidden the hole from him. He was once again filled with irrational anger and it was consuming him.

I had to protect Victor. I knew he was about to get one hell of a beating. Not only would it physically hurt him, but also it would tear me up again inside for not being able to stop it. I sent Victor out of the room so I could quell the situation. I told Tim that Victor had lived in fear for the last few days because he knew how mad his father would be and how pissed off at him he would be. I then told him that I believed that was enough of a punishment for him. To my great surprise and relief, Tim agreed. Instead of turning from Jekyll to Hyde he went from Hyde to Jekyll. Victor had to pay for the supplies and repair the whole himself. That was a reasonable consequence, one, rarely seen in our house.

If Tim was sick he was miserable. I had to wait on him hand and foot on top of doing everything else that was expected of me. He had a hernia and had to have surgery. He was getting in and out of bed moving kind of funny. He was sore and couldn't move properly. I was helping him and laughed at the way he was moving. He yelled at me and told me I was being insensitive for laughing at him because he was hurting. I wasn't laughing at him just at the way he was moving and it wasn't meant to hurt him as he deliberately did to us so many times.

Sometimes he was actually funny to be around but that was once in a blue moon. He even thought up a game that we would play at supper but it had to be done with his type of music and his rules. He would put on a concert by Mozart or big band music and we would then think of whom the music reminded us. If the drums were playing we could picture one of the aunts stomping down the hall or if bells were ringing we could picture one of the little cousins flitting around the room laughing. Who we pictured would depend on the music because the music had to fit the person's personality.

We even did pajama runs in the summer. The children would be put to bed then a little while later he would go into their rooms and say pajama run. We would go to the ice cream dairy shop with the children in their pajamas. We would get sundaes or ice cream cones and take pleasure in the nice summer night, one of the few joys he bestowed upon us.

We had a beautiful dog. She was a purebred Maltese, sable color with just a touch of black on the end of her tail. The gentlest and most beautiful dog a family could have. Kally was well behaved and would not leave the boundaries of the yard unless she was told she could. If Tim was in a bad mood even the dog had to watch out. He would kick her and sometimes he would actually pick her up and throw her. Kally would cower in a corner for hours. When she would come back out, her tail would be between her legs. She would crawl on the floor towards him and want his attention. As if nothing happened he would pet her and show her his kind of love.

One thing that was not changeable was his control. Though Jekyll would come out and be caring, Hyde would always be there to control all that we did. He wanted control in everything, even in what I was to wear.

We were invited to a dance at the base it was Valentine's Day. I had on a red dress with string straps and a little jacket over it. Tim told me I looked nice, *but* he wanted me to wear an old pink sweater over it and to get a chain for my glasses and wear them hanging down in front of me like a little old lady. I had to wear the sweater but refused to wear the glasses.

We were on the dance floor and he had been in a pretty good mood. He swung me around and twisted my arm. I let out a yell because of the pain it caused. His mood changed in an instant. There was rage written all over his face, Hyde was in his eyes once again and I knew I was in a lot of trouble. He told me to shut up and lower my voice and when we got home, I was screamed at over and over again. "How dear you embarrass me in front of the people I work with?" "Don't you know I have to go to work and deal with those people?" "You better keep your mouth shut and don't you ever disgrace and humiliate me again."

We were going out with Moe and his girl friend Jan one night. Tim had been in a dark mood for the millionth time. He wanted to drive which showed his need to be in charge. I was struggling to get the car seat out of the back seat and wasn't doing it fast enough. He was livid, because it wasn't being removed quickly enough in his opinion. He leaned over the seat and screeched at me to hurry and get the damn car seat out of the car. He humiliated me in front of our two friends. He kept at me all night with little digs here and there incessantly. Talking to them Jekyll was there but every time he looked at me, I was facing Hyde.

I heard Jan say to Moe that she was going to say something to Tim about his behavior towards me. Moe told her not to say a word because it would only make it worse for me once they left. Jan had only been over a few times and she was mortified at his treatment of me. After that she rarely came to visit. She felt her hands were tied and could not stand to watch his treatment of the children and me.

Moe and Jan were great friends and our situation affected them both differently. Unlike Jan, Moe came over all the time. Once a decision was made that Tim and I would separate, Jan wrote a letter to our confused, angry and fearful son.

Jan's letter to Victor

Dear Victor,

Moe told me today about your mom and dad's separation. My thoughts immediately go out to Marti and most of all, to you. You are home where most of the tension is centered. If you ever need to talk and know it will not go anywhere else, just call me or e-mail me. I am a good listener.

A long time ago I met Moe and I found a great person, so true to himself and everyone else. He truly cares for everyone he knows. He so understands and will listen to everything you have to say and keeps things to himself. He also gives so much of himself to all those he loves. I met your mom and dad before I met Moe's family. I should have gotten the clue then that the Dudleys were as much his family as his mom and dad were. He liked going over there a lot. He loved you and your sister so very much. We could not go over there without you and Marti taking him by the hand for a visit with each of you, to have your own special time with Uncle Moe, playing a game or reading a story.

I know a few things about raising children (not much but a few) and I know children need discipline and that starts at home. I know that the harshest punishments are given out when no one else is around (in the privacy of a house), but a house is not a home unless there is a mixture of discipline, love, tenderness, caring, giving and taking.

At first Moe and I spent a lot of time with your mom, dad and, you and your sister, but as time went on and I saw things happening at your house that started to upset me. I have trouble keeping my big mouth shut and sometimes my emotions build and I say things that are not my place to say. I always wanted to make things better, but some people look at it as "sticking my nose where it doesn't belong." I often spoke to Moe about my feelings and he asked me to stay out of other people's business. He didn't think giving my opinion would do any good and may only make things worse. Because of my love for Moe I agreed to stay out of things and in time I could see that he was right. He also understood I had to put some distance between myself and a situation I could not change. So my visits to your house were fewer over the past years. Moe didn't talk to me about the problems there, and I tried to understand his need to visit as often as he could. He thought his being there would keep some calm and provide a sounding board for all of you. That is what he wanted to accomplish the most during his visits. I hope his presents will always be a comfort for you and your family and I hope you all understand his good intentions.

There is a saying you should learn "time heals all" but what does it mean? There is never a good time for a family to break up but I think that now is the time to be happy. It takes a long time, a lot of hurt and pain to come to the point and the decision to make it all stop. The break up needs to happen before the happiness can come. Your family has had a lot of hurt and a lot of pain and someone in your family has made a good decision that it is time for it to stop. It will never be as it was before and maybe in time you will see that as a good thing. You need the true happiness to start. Perhaps in time your parents can resolve their differences and get back together; if that is the best for both of them. Or it may be that they both will be happier apart, but you need to let them decide their own future. As for you, you will always have both of them, together or apart. During this period they will go through hard times. They are both hurt in so many ways and they are both afraid of so many things they cannot share with anyone. They will both say and do things they normally would not do, because they are in a situation they have never been in before. It is just as confusing for them as it is for you and Marti. The biggest thing they are both afraid of is that you and Mari will not love them anymore. They both want to hold on to all the love they can. They need all the love the two of you can give. Share your love and try not to become judgmental or opinionated. Sharing you love will be the hardest job you will ever have, but one that will enrich the rest of your life. Happiness will be yours.

Whenever you need to talk always remember there is someone at 555-xxxx who is waiting for your call, and we know that time will heal, but in the meantime you may want to talk about it with someone who cares about you.

All my love,

Jan

Jan gave this letter to my son after she found out that Tim and I separated. She wanted Victor to know that there was indeed someone he could rely on. Victor knew that he could not count on his father or me. I was too wrapped up in having freedom for the first time in 19 years, and his father was too busy drinking. Victor did take Jan up on her offer one night when his father got drunk.

The next time I saw Jan after she gave my son this letter I hugged her tight and cried. We talked for a long time. Over the years I felt she didn't like me and resented Moe's and my relationship. He and I were, and still are, very best friends. Whenever we called he was there for us no questions asked. Sometimes he spent more time at our house than with her in his own home. She explained that she just could not stand coming over and being a witness to the constant abuse that was occurring in our house. And when she did come over she felt very uncomfortable. As I look back, I could feel it in her.

When she did come over; she would give Tim digs, especially about his black truck. She knew he spent way too much money on it and knew I hated it. She would call it the dump truck, garbage truck and anything she could to get under his skin. But she did it in a way that we did not feel his fury later.

9. Chores

The children and I hated doing our chores. We knew if things were not perfect, we would have to do them over again. Not so much me, but definitely the children. I would have to help them frequently so they would not get into trouble, but even that would not always work. They knew if their father found one little thing wrong there would be a penalty to pay. No matter how perfect they did things, it was not to his satisfaction. Many times they would have to spend hours redoing what they just spent hours doing because they didn't want to spend yet more time doing their chores for a third and fourth time. Marti had to dust, vacuum, and wash the floors. The vacuuming had to be done first; it would stir up the dirt and dust. If she dusted first then vacuumed she would have to re-dust the furniture again because Tim felt it was now dirty from the dust that was stirred up. She had to wash and wax the floors too. With a wax can in one hand and a cloth in the other she would go over the floor. I checked her work making sure all spots were covered with wax. If Tim came in and found one tiny spot Marti missed, she would have to wash and wax the entire floor for a second time. Of course she would do this after he finished humiliating her, screaming at her and telling her what a lousy job she did. "What is the matter with you; can't you even wash and wax a floor without messing it up? You've done this a million times and you still can't do it right."

Victor would have to take out the trash, scour the bathroom and pick up the dog poop. As with his sister things had to be perfect. Victor, however, had to be ultimately perfect. If the bathroom was not done to

Tim's liking, he would literally throw Victor into the bathroom screaming at him, putting him down and telling him how useless he was. One day Victor was thrown into the shower doors so hard I thought they would shatter. The glass rattled in the door-frame and the metal of the doors slammed against its own frame. Victor was hurt, his leg hit the metal frame, and he immediately had a large bruise across it. He was limping and crying. Of course Tim started calling him a baby and then slapped him across the face. I screamed at Tim to stop. He started yelling at me to mind my own damn business. Adding that Victor was "just a mama's boy" and he needed to stop being a "wimp." I again pleaded with him to stop, but he would not. Once again Victor got into more trouble because I tried to intervene and stop the abuse being inflicted on him. When Tim was done having his tantrum, Victor would have to re-clean the bathroom whether he was injured or not.

I learned to outwit Tim with the bathroom. Once Victor scoured it I checked it for him and we would fix whatever was necessary. Then right before his father got home I would spray the heck out of the bathroom with disinfectant and wipe the sink and faucets down so it seemed ultra clean. Everything was shining and smelled clean when his inspection was made.

If Victor missed any dog poop, Tim would go get him, dig his fingers into the back of his neck and lead him outside to where the poop was. He would force Victor's face down near the poop all the while yelling at him telling him if he didn't pick it up right, he would make him do it with his hands. He would then shove Victor hard sending him to the ground. Tim would continue ranting at Victor and tell him to finish the job, complete with all the warnings and why he had better do it correctly. The trash wasn't usually a problem. The trash barrels were kept out back by the garage door. After a couple of times of animals getting into them and Victor paying the price, I went out and bought trash cans with locking lids on them. This way the animals couldn't tip over the barrels and I would save Victor from at least one extra beating a week. On trash day, Victor would take the barrels through the garage across the front yard to the road to be picked up.

One particular day, Tim came into the house swinging. He was furious. I didn't know what was going on. He then took Victor by the cuff of his shirt into the garage and shoved his face towards the truck showing him what he had done. Victor by accident ran one of the barrels down the side of the truck leaving scuff-marks. Tim was furious and out of control with rage. I followed him because I knew by the tone of his voice that my son was once again in danger. Victor got clobbered over and over again. I kept telling Tim it was an accident and begged him to stop hitting Victor, only to be told to back down. "Don't butt in Samantha or he will get it again." All I could do was stay close by riddled with fear and praying my son would be okay and that someday this would all end. All the time, pleading with him to stop that Victor was little and he was hurting him. Reminding Tim over and over again that he was just a small child and didn't know better; nothing ever worked. And when I did get between them Tim would shove me out of the way. He would not listen to me and as always Victor would get a worse beating because I would try to stop it. I started looking for a cover for his damn truck. I hated that truck. Tim spent too much money on it and my son paid the price for it. At last a cover was found. Now his precious truck would be protected from an innocent child doing his chores.

I had no self esteem after years of being put down and threatened I had no choice but to back down. I thought I was helping my son, but he would get belted an extra time each time I opened my mouth. Tim had threatened me so much, saying he would take the children from me that I believed I couldn't survive without him. I believed I wasn't good at anything; I was trapped. At the time, I thought I was doing what I could for the survival of my children. Each time he went after the children I would cringe, always hoping that they would be okay, especially Victor, who got it the most and the worst. I shed many, many tears over the years, praying that things would get better. They didn't, and no matter how much I begged and pleaded with Tim to stop, he didn't. Because of my "interfering" he belted, punched, poked or slapped Victor and Marti one more time. Many times I got in-between but Tim would push me out of the way and hit Victor again saying "that is for you and your big mouth"; telling him to stop crying and stop being a wimpy mama's boy. Tim said, women belong in the house and men belong outdoors. So the fall and winter months were mostly up to Victor for chores. In the fall Victor would have to rake the yard and get rid of the leaves. One gloomy fall day the right side of our yard was free of leaves. I told Victor don't worry about raking it. There was nothing to rake. Tim came home and of course had to inspect the yard. Seeing no rake marks on the right side of the yard, he called Victor out. I knew right away what was going to happen. I flew out the back door and told Tim it was my fault. I explained that I told Victor not to rake that one side because there were no leaves to rake. He screamed at me telling me not to get in the way of him chastising the kids on what they had to do. He then hit Victor, telling him it was for my "interfering" behavior once again. Victor then had to rake the entire yard over again and wasn't allowed to come in until it was done. His father didn't come home until around 5:15, so this meant that Victor wouldn't be done until long after dark. Victor also wouldn't be allowed to have supper until it was done. I begged and pleaded with Tim to let him come in and have supper. To my great surprise he agreed but Victor had to go right back out after supper to finish the yard. I wanted to go out and help him as it was my fault he got into trouble, but Tim refused to let me. He controlled me. Victor also had to clean out under the deck. It was about 20 feet long by 12 feet wide. It would always be filled with leaves, dirt, bugs and spiders. Victor hated it, his father would make him crawl underneath the deck and pull all the leaves out. It would take Victor a long time to creep around underneath the deck to be sure it was clean. It was a dirty job and Victor was not happy about doing it, but did it just the same. He knew he would feel his father's wrath if he complained about not liking or wanting to do this chore.

When it snowed, Victor not only had our driveway to do but his grandparents' driveway as well. Regardless of the freezing cold New England weather when Victor finished our driveway. He had to go down the street and do their driveway. Both had better be perfect, scraped right down to the black top and done before his father got home from work. Tim learned his irrational behavior from his father. His father was even more particular about things being done perfectly than Tim was. One day I was over helping the in-laws do the driveway. Mrs. D. didn't have the corner done exactly as specified. Mr. D. got mad and threw a shovel full of snow at her, yelling at her as he did so. I took Victor with me and left. I had enough yelling and screaming at my own house, I didn't need to listen to them. Sometimes Victor didn't get the driveway done because he had to go to school. I would start doing the driveway if Victor couldn't get it done; always trying to ensure he would not get another beating. Sometimes I would not be able to help. It was hard, because I had a home day care at this time and parents would show up between 6:30 and 7 o'clock in the morning. I couldn't go out and leave the children alone, to help Victor. On the really frigid days, the snow would freeze by the time Victor got home from school. The condition of the driveway would inevitably not be up to his father's satisfaction because he had been unable to chop the ice and shovel the driveway. Tim would come home and Victor of course got verbally abused and belted around. I felt that I was doomed to be the buffer between Tim and Victor just as Mrs. D. had been between Tim and his father. Not a job I enjoyed, especially, because Victor would get the extra punch, slap, shove or verbal put down because I "interfered" on his behalf.

10. Hide and Seek

I hated my life. I always had to think of ways to protect the children and try to outsmart their father. Things continued to get worse. There was so much friction between us, that all we did was yell at each other. I was on pins and needles continually and didn't know if I was coming or going. Marti and Victor didn't know love in this house; all they knew were fits of rage, temper tantrums, hollering, emotional and physical abuse. They were not happy and they couldn't stand each other. That only made it worse. When they were very young I would tell Tim if they gave me a hard time. I was looking for moral support, understanding and ideas on how to handle various situations; after all, Tim was their father. If I could not ask him for help then who could I ask? That quickly stopped because he would reprimand them harshly. Even if I scolded them or punished them for the day, he would punish them again. I stopped telling him if things went wrong and that only made our situation worse. I couldn't tell him what happened and if he did find out then I was in big trouble. But at least in the beginning the children didn't get into trouble. Tim was more into putting me down and asserting his control over me that he paid little attention to the children. As the children grew, they realized mom would do anything for them; and they played on that. They would not listen to me at all. They knew that they would get in trouble all the same when their father got home, so why listen to mom. They didn't dare have a hair out of place with their father. The limits were set and they didn't challenge or step outside his boundaries. They were well aware that if they did, they would surely pay the consequences for their actions.

Because I was always trying to compensate for their father's brutality, I didn't imposed restrictions. Everything goes haywire without boundaries or a guidance system. By over compensating out of love, the children only suffered more. I could not stand the thought of them not loving me; their love was all I had to hold on to. It would devastate me if they didn't love me, so they got away with anything and everything. Unknowingly, I enabled them to use things against me. I knew that it was my fault. I let them down, I wanted a happy home for them, but it didn't exist. I wanted to make up for the misery, heartache and fear their father was putting them through. I believed that by giving in to them that it would make things a little happier for them. All I wanted was for my children to be happy and to laugh. I didn't want them to worry about paying a high price for their actions. Just to be a kid, that is what they needed to do, not be afraid to breathe in their own house or be fearful of their father. I wanted to look at their faces and see joy in their eyes, not fear. All I could see was the emptiness and **bitterness** that held them **hostage** in the house they lived in and hated. I detested Tim, I believed him when he said that I was no good at anything. I never had the house clean enough, wasn't good in bed, couldn't control the children, couldn't do things quick enough, was never able to make a good enough meal without him complaining about it and the list goes on and on with no signs of any change. Things just kept getting worse and I didn't know what to do or were to turn. I was isolated and had no friends, except for Moe. Many days he came over to check on us and I would just vent to him and sometimes cry on his shoulder. In our house, without looking at the clock we knew automatically when it was 4:30. It was as if a light turned on every day, we knew Tim would be home soon and things had better be right; but they never were. Every day I would go around frantically cleaning and getting things in perfect order to lessen the effects of Tim's temper when he came through the door.

The children were told they had to go to their rooms to do homework right after school, but often times I would let them outside to play because I knew they would not have a chance later. If they got grounded for weeks, I let them out when their dad wasn't around. It was the only freedom they had. I can only imagine how much these inconsistencies affected them. Many times I took the blame for what the children did so they wouldn't get beaten by their father. I knew that I would get yelled at, threatened or get dirty digs; I knew the children would be hit, ridiculed, grounded or worse.

One afternoon the children were in the kitchen fighting. Victor had the super glue and was trying to fix something and Marti was trying to order him around. He got mad and slammed the glue on the counter causing it to explode. Glue splattered all over the counter and our new kitchen floor. Immediately fear engulfed all of us. The color drained from the kids faces as they stood there shaking, because dad was due home at any moment. Never mind the glue everywhere, they knew that if their father found out they were fighting, all hell would break loose. Victor knew he would get a beating. Marti knew she would get the inevitable poke in the chest and both of them knew they would be grounded on top of the grounding they were already serving. I knew what to expect and knew they were in the same panic mode.

We tried cleaning up the glue but couldn't, we were able to scrape it off the counter, but the floor was a soft tile and the glue ate right into it. It was too late, the tiles were already damaged.

Victor would get the shit kicked out of him, so I would tell their father I did it. I made up some story about fixing a cup and dropped the glue and told Tim that it broke open when it hit the floor. Naturally, he told me how stupid I was and yelled at me because the floor was ruined. To me it was worth it. My children didn't suffer this time at the hands of their father. Naive, I was. I thought we got away with it, *Wrong!* Since Victor and I could no longer have a private or rational conversation I e-mailed him and told him he would have to pay to replace the tiles in the kitchen. I told him it was between he and I and his father wouldn't find out. I thought it was under control.

Tim came to me a few days later and told me that he knew all about it. He had read Victor's e-mail; *he had been reading all of our e-mail messages for quite some time.* I told the children their father was reading all our messages, and told them to be careful what they wrote. It was just one more way Tim had to ensure he had control of everything. I was shocked when Victor and Marti didn't feel his fury on this one. Victor still had to pay for the floor tiles. It was me that had hell to pay. Tim told me that I was a liar and couldn't be trusted. After all his put downs, he then gave me the cold shoulder for days. In retrospect, that was okay with me. I tried to talk to Tim about why I lied and took the blame. He didn't want to hear anything; that I was trying to protect the children. They got what they deserved, and I was stupid.

Marti and Victor were really beginning to hate each other; they never did anything together and blamed each other for the continued turmoil in which they lived. They had horrific fights and were going at each other with fists and snide remarks. Yelling, screaming and pounding on each other is how they communicated with each other. They learned from the hell they grew up in. One afternoon they were in the living room fighting. Marti shoved her brother into my floor length glass cabinet; his whole body fell into it. Crash, the glass completely shattered. It was a good thing that his boot hit the door and broke the glass first; otherwise his back would have gotten severely cut which would have landed him in the hospital. I attempted to see if he was all right but he just pushed me out of his way. The only thing flowing through him was fear, anger and rage. He took off without letting me see his injuries as tears slid down his face. He was terribly upset. I sent Marti's boyfriend after him. They were gone an extremely long time and I was getting really worried. I didn't know if my son was hurt, bleeding or if John even found him. As Marti and I waited for them to return she was screaming about her brother and how mad he made her. She blamed him for what happened. When they came back, John told me how mad Victor was and how he let Victor pound his fist against his chest. Victor stood there shaking and wailing away on him getting some of his anger out, all the time crying. John knew what was going on in our hell house and wanted to help but couldn't. I always begged people not to tell. Yet another person that got caught into our web of brutality and deceit; he didn't tell anyone a thing. Tim made our living hell worse than it already was whenever anything was said to him. He would always threaten that the state would take my children from me if anyone knew what went on at 1 Mitchell Drive.

We were in the living room cleaning up slivers of glass, petrified of what Tim would do when he saw the glass door smashed. We knew that we had to come up with something quick as he was due home shortly. We needed a plan. Marti agreed that she would say she was dusting. Instead of using a chair she was standing on the rocking chair and it rocked forward. With her weight on the rocker it hit the glass door and broke it. We were as usual on pins and needles until he came home. We knew that if he didn't believe what we said he was going to lose it and even though Marti did it and would get into trouble, Victor would pay the price. It is an interesting dynamic to look back at to see how Marti, angry at Victor, would herself be willing to take the blame for him. I think it speaks to the dysfunctionality and brutality that pervaded our family. I sent the children to their rooms, so I could tell their father what happened. He was mad of course, but neither of the children got screamed at or hit. We did it. We got away with it this time. We could breathe again. One less beating and one less session of berating was our reward on this day. Many times I took the blame if something got broken after the children had a fight. I knew if I took the blame, they would not get hit. I would face the music and take the snide remarks and belittling instead of them. To me it was worth it time and time again. Any little thing would set Tim off. We never knew what would be the trigger or how or when the explosion would occur. If I went to the store, when I came home, I would find the children in their rooms in tears. And usually Victor would have gotten hit and they were both grounded again. So it reached a point where I tried never to leave the children home with their father. It was much safer that way. They knew I would buy them an extra treat when they were with me. They knew how to play the guilt card and make me feel guilty causing me to concede getting them an extra snack. Always they were told not to tell their father. It would put a smile on their faces for a little while. It was worth it to me and I didn't mind spending a little extra money on them to put a little happiness into their bleak dreary lives.

By the time Victor was in second grade he was getting a slap in the face or upside the head every day. I felt helpless. Tim had successfully made me believe that he would take my children from me. He always told me that I couldn't prove a thing. He threatened me all the time. My children were everything to me, so in my own way I did what I could for them. Trying to protect them, taking the blame if something got broken, helping them with their chores and the list goes on.

I realized something had to be done. Marti came home from school and told me she was called into the office and asked about some red marks on Victor's face. Even my daughter was hiding everything. She told the nurse that she and her brother were wrestling and she pushed his face into the carpet and it was a rug burn. They bought it. Marti was such a sweet kid in school and very good so why wouldn't they believe her? With everything going on in the house, now she gets called into the office and has to lie to protect her brother. She told me she was so frightened they would take her and Victor away. I told her I would do anything and everything to make sure that would not happen. I was so pissed off and felt so sorry for her. But what could I do? So as always, I covered up again and again and again for the children. Tim's threats constantly over my head, fearing for my children, he knew they meant the world to me and he used it to control me.

He always said that things were closing in on him. That was one of his ways to keep me in line. He would tell me if things didn't get better he would leave and take the kids and I would have nothing. The walls were closing in because of the mess in the house, the children not behaving (gee *I wonder why!)* and I wasn't good enough in any way. It the state of mind I was in and truly believed in I would once again try to improve myself and the conditions of our everyday lives. But because of Tim and his expectations of me I would not be successful.

I hated my life increasingly, but stayed for the children. I thought back then that it was the right thing to do. I would do anything for them even if it meant his degrading treatment and non consensual sex. That way at least he would be in an okay mood for a little while and the children wouldn't hit another snag. I believed they needed their father and a family, but I know now that I should have taken my children and left him many years before. The secrets I kept only made our hell last longer. Instead of being grateful to some teacher who cared and noticed my son was in trouble, I could only think of covering up.

11. Counseling

When my son was in second grade his teacher called me in for a conference. He was becoming unruly and misbehaving in class. He would get up in the middle of the room, throw his crayons on the floor and stomp on them; he wouldn't pay attention and would bother the other students. She thought it was Attention Deficit Hyper Disorder (ADHD). I went along with it and had him tested. It did turn out Victor was ADHD. Here was a perfect way to hide some of what was behind his behavior. We went to a counselor for him, *which* his father did not support and thought was a "crock." Counselors are worthless; they just want your money and don't know what they are talking about. That was Tim's take on it. The counselor was told a limited version of the terrible events that went on. He agreed that because of the ADHD that some of the trouble could be stopped once we learned Victor's behavioral patterns and how to handle them. He truly believed that most of the trouble could be fixed. I took hold of this full force, wanting nothing more than the fighting, yelling, beatings and abuse to stop. Victor went to the counselor once a week. He never talked about it. Even at eight years old he needed someone to trust and to confide in. He could tell his counselor whatever he wanted and so he did. It helped him for a short while.

One night we showed up at the counselor's office for our session. I was in tears after another of Tim's put-downs. The counselor told Tim that to help the situation we needed to get along and that he needed to treat me better. Tim needed to stop putting me down, stop making me cry, and needed to treat me with respect. Although Tim listened, he did not, as usual, hear what the counselor had said to him. He took me out to dinner after the meeting and later that night his idea of making me feel better was to have humiliating sex. *Whoopee*. On this particular night, his idea of being intimate was oral sex. I just cried. I didn't want to have sex and it was degrading to me. He didn't know what it was to be intimate nor did he have any idea what I needed that night. To him being intimate was sex and anything to do with it no matter what kind of sex it was. What I needed at that point was just to sit or lay together, cuddling in each others' arms. Just holding and listening to the other person's breath and maybe a soft kiss once in a while and talking, really talking. And listening in such a way so as to actually *hear* what the other person was saying. Not just nodding to what was being said, then letting it go in one ear and out the other, making believe that listening was actually taking place. Being in my husband's arms should have been a safe place for me, but it was not. It was a terrifying place, a dreaded place full of fear and turmoil. I never knew when he would blow and Hyde would come out again. What I knew would be coming was not pleasant or reassuring to me. It was frightful and hurtful all the time. It was not loving it was forced sex. Even if we were not in the bedroom, if he would hug me it was with sex in mind. His hands would go into my shirt or down my pants to indicate what he had on his mind, which was sex 24/7. Counseling did nothing for us; it helped with our son for a short while and gave me a little courage to speak up once in a while in order to try to protect my son and daughter.

One day, Marti said. "What about me?" I asked the counselor if he felt she needed to be seen. He did see her a few times. He said she was doing okay, so I didn't worry much about Marti and how she was doing but; she was not okay. Marti was a lot worse than any of us knew and more than she ever let on. A few years later I put her into counseling with a different therapist. We had to read the rules and policies and sign it knowing that if the therapist found any abuse, she would have to report it to the authorities. At home that night I told Marti she could talk about anything she wanted except the abuse that went on in our house. I told her that she and her brother would be taken from me if the therapist found out what was happening in our house of doom. I could not bear the thought of losing them. It was drilled into my head and I believed whole-heartedly that Tim would take my precious children from me. Marti agreed not to mention the abuse and went to therapy for a while. In retrospect although I arranged for the counseling to occur, I prevented her from getting the help she needed. This was exactly what I did not want to do. That, in and of itself, speaks to the sick control Tim had over me. Because of what Tim drilled into my head about taking the children away from me, I unknowingly hurt my daughter. Even though she couldn't stand her brother she had also become his protector, just as I was their protector. While I thought I was protecting my family by keeping our dirty secrets I was unknowingly doing more harm to Marti. I didn't know how much it would eat away at my daughter and how much guilt and hurt she would carry around with her for a very long, long time. She was afraid and in fear and I couldn't do a damn thing about it.

As we drove to the therapist for her session I again drilled into her head what she could and could not talk about. My daughter looked at me with hatred in her eyes as if I were a different person, her father. I was possessed with Tim's words for fear of losing my children and speaking what was wired into my being. It wasn't me speaking but his words through me. Marti knew this and hated me for it. Where was I even though I was saying those threatening words, lost in a world of total depression, isolation and continual fear? I wished desperately that Marti would reveal the abuse to the therapist. The dreaded secret would be out and we could get some help. The beatings would stop, the gloom would disappear and the children would eventually smile again. But I knew it would not happen. We were in constant fear and knew if we stepped out of line all hell would break out. The proverbial fist would drop hard and leave another damaging physical or emotional scare.

I was always trying to protect my children at all cost; not realizing the real cost it would have on them. I felt guilty for telling her what she could talk about, but as always, Tim had control. He set down the rules for her to go and if he didn't like the way she was behaving after therapy she wouldn't be allowed to go anymore. He had control over everything we did every day, every minute and every second of every day. I didn't know better - I was scared to death, depressed, and thought I was doing the right thing at the time. In my thinking some therapy for Marti was better than none. I had nothing left of myself. I had no self-esteem and was afraid to breathe the wrong way. I knew I didn't do anything right and was put down time after time no matter what it pertained to. I was a useless and worthless person. I live with the guilt of the past every day of my life. I know that I did the best I could for the situation I was dealing with; however it doesn't make me feel any better about what my children had to go through and what they are still dealing with today.

I tried reading some self help books, but I could never get through them. Until now it has been very painful to bring up the past and deal with it. All I did was cry each time I would start a chapter in a book. Cried so hard because of so much hurt and pain that I couldn't see the writing on the pages and shook so much that I couldn't hold a pencil to write. Now unfortunately the books sit on a shelf with the pages marked collecting dust.

I even tried religion as a form of counseling for myself. I went to church every Sunday with or without my family and truly enjoyed going to mass. My favorite hymn was and still is, "Let There Be Peace on Earth."

I used to pray for stupid things when I was young, like winning a million dollars or a beautiful vacation, a nice house and a perfect family. But as I grew and life continued to get more difficult, I knew the more important thing to pray for was the safety of my children. And I continued praying, though my belief was increasingly tempered by a hopeless realization that each day - no matter how hard I prayed - my son would still get the shit kicked out of him. For years I kept praying harder and harder, pleading with the Lord to help us and make the pain and suffering go away. It never did.

In my eyes, God is supposed to be all-knowing and all-powerful. If this is true, then *why did He let the abuse go on for so long*? With his all mighty powers, He should have been able to stop all the destruction that was going on in our house of misery. Many people say God has His reasons for letting things happen as they do. I will never understand how he could let two precious little children continue to get abused and mistreated for so long and do nothing about it. As with everything else I tried, I now had no hope and no faith to help me though the horrific times we endured. I just couldn't believe in anything anymore.

Because of my lack of good judgment, as well as my insecurities and foggy mind, I never noticed that Marti was no longer going to therapy after about six months in. I wouldn't find out until years later that she was afraid to keep going. The therapist was getting too close to what was really going on and Marti didn't want her to know, she didn't want to be taken away. She was terribly afraid for her family. Marti felt she had no one to confide in and was depressed, miserable, lonely, and sad. Because of my own inabilities, I was unable to see or recognize my own traits that had now become hers. Marti was becoming a younger version of me, and she would hide our hideous secret with every ounce of strength she had in her.

12. Attention and Playtime

Tim didn't give the children any positive attention. I would read to Marti every night when she was little. Her favorite story was Disney, "The Sorcerer's Apprentice." When Victor was old enough I would read to them both. Victor didn't care what story it was as long as the three of us sat together on one of their beds sharing the time. But like everything else, Tim wanted control of this too. So before the children reached the ages of four and five reading to them before bed was banned. Tim felt it was a waste of time.

Once they were in school, I provided all the homework help and attended the school functions. I was to nurture, bathe, soothe and comfort them. Playing was limited because we were always doing things to try to please Tim. So much of that time could have been spent on just having fun, learning and loving experiences.

The attention Tim did give Victor was 99% negative. Victor picked up on this. He understood very early that if I want my dad's attention, I just need to do something wrong. This made things much worse. Victor learned to push Tim's buttons, and he would inevitably pay dearly for it; but he got the attention. Victor could do the littlest thing like talk during a TV show, drop a spoon, not put things away exactly the right way or in the correct spot and all hell would break loose. Victor would end up getting hit, kicked, pushed, thrown, sworn at; or whatever Tim deemed fit for the offense committed by a little kid.

Every time I saw that look in Tim's eyes or heard the tone of his voice, I would cringe. I knew the children were in for it and the battle would start. I usually stood very close, trying to keep Tim at arm's length in order to protect the children. I always stood there trembling, not knowing what was coming. I guess I knew what was coming, but to what extent the result would be each time I didn't know. I would always plead with Tim to back off and not hit the children, but I was always told not to interfere with the way he disciplined "his" kids. Funny, I did everything else, the only time they were "his" kids was when it came to disciplining them. Tim did start showing the children some *false* positive attention when they were a little older. Usually it would be after supper; our so-called play time. Tim felt that was our quality time. He would go sit and watch TV while the children and I would clean; he never helped us. After the dishes were done, the table wiped and the floor swept he would say "daddy's tired." He would then go lie on our bed and make believe he was sleeping. The children would run into the bedroom, jump on him and they would wrestle.

There were many times the children got hurt, landing on the floor or bruised, but they always wanted to play. Once, Victor had his elbow dislocated during playtime. This, I think, was an indication of how rough he was with the children. The children never won either, but it remained the only time dad would play with them; and they were starving for his attention. Little did they know, at the time, that they would never win and that playtime would always be on his terms. This, in my opinion was just another way that he would always have the upper hand and maintain control. I always made sure that I went in to watch, after realizing early-on, how rough the wrestling actually was. The children would often say, "Come-on mom," but I said I just liked watching them. To please the children I joined in a few times, but always got an arm-twisted, knocked off the bed or hit in some (*accidental)* way. So he said. It hurt no less. He pushed me so brutally hard one time that I slammed into the foot-board of the bed and broke the solid six-inch crossbar in two. Of course Tim was mad that the bed was broken, but we didn't get into trouble that night. I think he actually realized that he did the pushing and caused it to happen. The bed never got fixed. Knowing he had the control and could hurt Victor and Marti at anytime always put me on guard. They didn't know that I was their guard and protector; I would jump in if I saw that things were getting really rough and I thought that the children would get hurt. This way he could take out his aggression on me and not them. I was stronger than they were, and I could take more abuse than they could. I could at least fight back; I never won, but I could protect them and protect them I did - whatever the cost. I stood there watching them over and over again, laughing and playing with their dad and loving the little attention they were getting from him. But as I stood there watching, it was with a heavy heart and a morbid dread that his mood would change, Hyde would return. The children would inevitably be in trouble and get hit again. I was on guard, always watching for little signs that Tim was changing. If I saw a sign, for instance if the children would get a good lick in, he would get upset. I would jump in to divert the attention to myself. That way Tim would be more likely not to take it out on them.

Towel snapping was another one of Tim's favorite games to play. The four of us would each have a towel and try to snap the other person first without getting snapped back. The dog didn't like towel snapping. She would bark and bark, and if you weren't looking she would grab the towel out of your hand and run with it. I was glad because Tim knew he couldn't play without another person or without Kally constantly barking. Kally was the easiest going dog ever, never a growl or show of teeth, the gentlest dog around. Even she knew how rough he could be and wanted to protect the three of us. She would snatch the towel right out of Tim's hand to keep him from hitting us with it. I played this one. I *had* to. Tim never let up; he always had to be triumphant. It didn't matter that he was playing with two small children. He was in the "Towel Game" to win and that was that. With me playing, it kept him off the children for a little while longer.

I got exceptionally well at striking him and backing out of the way of his return. Being small, and with the protective instinct I had for my children it made me quick. Because I was 60 pounds lighter than Tim, I was able to move in quickly and retreat. I learned to be quick, to defend against him and outwit him. I would position myself on his left side: Tim was right handed. Then I would snap quickly and sharp always keeping his attention on me and not the children. Once Tim was snapped, I would move in quick, right up next to him. He wouldn't be able to snap at me, because he had no room to move. He would get so mad and frustrated with me that he would shove me away violently, so that he could snap. But, I was right back in next to him, already snapping and moving back in. Tim didn't like this at all, he would get extremely aggravated because he could not lash out and have control at that moment. He would go for the open skin of our hands. It hurt and burned tremendously. I learned to snap with a long sleeve shirt on, or with the towel wrapped around my hand. This was my way of getting back at him for all the mistreatment of the children and me - and without him knowing that it was being done. If he ever knew that I was knowingly getting the upper hand, heaven help me, there would be no surviving. He was that kind of a calculating person. One who had to prove he was the boss and had to be in command of all situations at all times. He wasn't the only one in the service, we all were, and we had to survive; out maneuver him was the key, which infuriated him, all the more. I paid a price when he learned I had the upper hand, even if it was for only a minute. He could never loose, not to a woman, especially not to his wife; someone who in his eyes, was not on equal ground with him. Sometimes Tim would get quite irritated and drive me to the ground hard, so he had time to continually snap before I could get up. This way he could be in be control again. He could never be out of control. He always had to win. He always had to be right. If he went after the children, I would go after him, because I knew he wouldn't hold back with them and eventually they would get hurt. I still don't think they recognized how much I tried to protect them and how much hurt and discomfort I saved them from. In spite of my efforts they still had a lot of pain and suffering. If we got snapped on bare skin it would sting and hurt. It would bring tears to our eyes and ultimately would leave big red welts, bruises and swelling on our bodies.

One day, I was really pissed off at Tim. I was tired of his put downs and his criticizing the children and me relentlessly. I wanted to hurt him like he had hurt us so many times, but I knew without a doubt that if I punched him, talked back to him, or acted out in any way, the children would ultimately pay for it. Before he came into the room, I wet the end of the towel. Believe me if you got snapped with a wet towel, you knew it. It would leave a raised welt on your skin and it stung for a long time. I got away with it a few times, then one day he grabbed the towel in a huff, because I was beating him at the dumb game. This was the one game that I thought I could beat him at. He felt the wet end of the towel and was pissed off, but instead of screaming like he usually did, he wet his towel and I was in for it. He even tried to go for the children, but I was to be the blocker at all times. I had to protect my troops, my precious little children, who never asked to be in *his* war. He was not going to get to them, if I could help it. He came at me with a vengeance, striking and pushing without a sign that he was being merciless to his wife. Red-faced rage is all that was in him now. I fought with all I could, but he was relentless. No remorse. I was a soldier at war and I was determined that he would feel the hurt as well. Snapping and snapping, springing back and in again, time after time. My muscles ached, but eventually, the burning stopped. Tim's anger died down, but not without leaving me with large welts all over my body. Again I was made to believe that this outburst of his was my fault! I should not have wet the towel. I felt that I had no other way to speak out or defend the children and myself. I thought if I could do some tactical maneuvering of my own, without his knowing, I would feel a little better. I believed that knowing that I did one thing right, and that was to get the upper hand for once, I would feel better. I was wrong. It only made me feel more inadequate and less of a person. He won the battle again, put me down and wailed on me letting me know that he would always have absolute power. I failed my children once again. There was no triumphant moment.

We could not even go for a walk, without it being on his terms. The children and I would find a rock and take turns kicking it down the street trying to keep the same rock for our two mile walk. When Tim went with us we had to just walk, no rocks, no fun; just quiet, the way he required it to be. Walks eventually stopped as with anything else Tim didn't want to do or didn't think was to his benefit. At times, I believed my children hated me, because of all the yelling and because of what was going on. It was my fault for not being strong, so I thought. Tim made me believe it was my entire fault. Little did they know how very much I loved and wanted to protect them. Little did they know that I did everything that I could to accomplish just that.

13. Mother and Daughter Write

To My Daughter:

This is not written to hurt or

upset you, but hopefully to help.

A note to Marti...

First of all and most important, mommy loves you very much. I know you haven't been feeling good, but school is important. Besides you don't need to be home with me when all I do is yell at you. You know I am scared too that daddy will hurt you or me but especially Victor. He is only eight years old. Daddy is so much bigger and stronger. Last night daddy said he could beat Victor so bad and would not care. Daddy needs help and we need help from him. I'm also scared because I am telling you this. You are eleven years old and should not be going through this. You and Victor should be happy and having fun not being scared all the time. We always seem to have fun and are happy when daddy is gone away to school. I know you have trouble with friends. Maybe it is because you are so upset all the time. I wish you weren't. It is not fair for you and your brother to live this way. Just remember someone has it worse. Please don't ever run away. *I need you.* You give me strength to go on. I live for you and Victor. Marti, the two of you are so important to me. I wish I could make things better. I just don't know how. I'm afraid to talk to anyone because daddy will get mad if he finds out. That is why I am writing to you. I don't like to because it is not fair to put this all on you. You are just a little girl. But maybe if I write and let you know my feelings, you will understand. And maybe we can start getting along better. I don't like the way we have been lately. Also I'm writing because I know you like to get notes, but mostly because we seem to just fight when we talk lately. This way I can say what I want. You can read this and do what you want with it. I only hope it helps you. I have never done this before. I want you to know I care enough to write this to you. Make sure you destroy this letter.

I LOVE YOU

MOMMY

Years later this was so hard for me to read. I cried when I found these letters to my daughter and her diary. I cried so much at first I couldn't see what was written on the pages. I cried with relief knowing that I was not crazy and that it was in reality truly that bad a situation. I cried for my children who were robbed of their precious childhood and who would never get it back. I cried because of the demons they would have to face in the future to overcome what was dealt them, at the hand of their father. I cried for feeling like a failure, but now I know that Tim was to blame. Now I can start on the long road to healing. And I cried with relief knowing that I can go on and that there is proof of what this monster that was supposed to love us, did to us. Looking back and knowing how bad it was for the children and not having been able to do anything about it, is difficult. At times I thought maybe *it was* just me, not being good enough. At times I thought maybe it was not as bad as I thought it was. So many times I doubted myself over the years. What was I doing so wrong that caused me to deserve what was happening to my sweet children and me? I back then, really felt that I deserved what was happening to me.

Marti and I couldn't be in the same room without screaming at each other. The tension was always so high that none of us could relax and we took it out on each other. I was the mom and I should have been able to stop the craziness and safeguard my children, but after reading these letters, I know I did the best I could at the time it was happening. I was dealing with a very bad situation and I didn't know up or down, right from left, happy from sad. Everything just merged together for me and eventually, I just went through the motions distraught, depressed and without hope. Silently, secretly I was dealing with a real monster. One that most people only hear about and would never suspect it could happen to them, or to someone in their family. I know that even though I said that I loved Tim back then, that I didn't. I was doing what I thought was right. I was brought up Catholic and was doomed to stay in the marriage, no matter what, for better or worse, sickness and in health till death. And there were times when I thought I would die to end it, but then there was Marti and Victor. How could I leave them? We got the worse of the vows. I didn't want the children to have a family that was torn apart. I would do anything to keep things together. It was what I was supposed to do. And so, with that in my head, and with the constant threats hanging over me, I was powerless to do anything about a very dreadful situation. Day in and day out my children paid dearly for this and I will always live with that guilt. Even though I know it was not my fault, that it was Tim's. I will always wish I could have been stronger. He is the one who gave out the abuse physically and emotionally. At times I really thought my son would be killed during one of his father's abusive rages. My mother and sister often commented about our situation and the fear they had concerning the welfare of the children. Many times they said how they hoped the next time they saw Victor it would not be in a *coffin*.

The abuse took its toll on all of us; I got so depressed that I was, by no means, a proper mother to my children. They needed someone to be there and protect them and love them, but I couldn't function. I was so beaten down and most times I just didn't care, except for the children. They were everything to me and I would do anything not to let their father get to them. I always lived with the threat of him taking my children from me. Over and over again the same threat he would take my children from me. He knew they were my life and he used that against me to keep me jumping at his will and keep me in line.

Marti's diary

3/15/91

I had a big fight with my mom over clothes and I said there's no one to look up to and she took it the wrong way this house has been full of tense for a long time an now all my mom does is yell. Dad is much better now better he is even doing things for and with Victor. I need help I am at fault I did it all I get Victor mad buy teasing him and that gets mom mad because we fight and she starts yelling. I like it when dad comes home because now he doesn't get mad all the time.

Well I'm back. Dad has been spending lots of time with Victor and I guess that's okay but I want to spend time with dad to, it's not fair. By, I'm going to talk to mom.

Yes, sometimes the children even hated me and I don't blame them. I was so tense all the time; it only took the slightest thing to set me off. I was always on edge, I allowed him to make me that way, and over and over again, the children took the brunt of it. The teasing my daughter talked of was just the beginning of their fights. Over time they really went after each other violently.

4/12/91

Hi Mom,

What's up? I feel weird in CCD today I don't know why. I just all of a sudden feel like crying. There is something bothering me but I don't know what it is. Why do I feel weird? Can you tell me? What is bothering me and why? Please just try to answer my questions! I am crying out for help of somebody anybody but nobody is helping me! I need help I need someone to talk to, spend more time with you! Maybe you could just sit there and listen to me practice flute. Or maybe we could just sit together playing a game in or we could even work on one of our patches in my Girl Scout book. Mom, I don't like coming to elementary school and they all hate me they all always ignore me. Maybe we could just take a bike ride or a walk around the block. I can't wait to go home. I want to go home now! But I guess I can't Well I'm running out of room I guess I better let you go. I don't want to though well I guess I better before I get caught by my teacher.

Your troubled daughter Marti

12/14/92

Well diary it's been almost a year since I've seen you. Well your right JFK isn't all that bad. I'm in 8th grade now. My best friend is Ronnie Combs. I love her a lot she is someone I can talk to and really relate to. Lately things have been awful. It really all started when dad went back to school.

He is pulling everything all over again. He's yelling, screaming and hitting all the time again. Only this time he isn't doing it to my brother he's doing it to me. I HATE him so much. I have cried so much that I don't have any tears left to cry with.

A Poem by Marti

~ *Betrayed* ~

Friends?

Maybe not?

One who's there,

One who's not,

One who cares,

Maybe not?

One to look to,

Then again?

Something to think about,

Are they real,

Are they trustworthy,

Maybe not?

Are they worth it,

Then again?

Think,

Why?

They don't care,

Why? Why? Do I?

That's the way I am,

Not the way they are,

Me, Myself, and I always alone,

Different values, different tastes,

Now I have it figured out,

They don't care why should I?

Even though there were four people living in the house and her grandparents were only two houses away, my daughter was so alone and scared. She had nowhere to turn and no one she could trust. Her parents had indeed betrayed her, her father with his abusive ways; and her mother, with no backbone to stand up to him. She was crying out for help and I couldn't see it past all the abuse that was keeping me held prisoner in my house and in my confused state of mind. She felt alone and forgotten and thought no one cared about her. I did care and I loved her with everything in me I just couldn't function. I had no will of my own. Tim stripped me of that and all the strength, the fight, the toughness, the will power and happiness that made up my being. It was all gone. I was an empty shell.

Yesterday, 12/15/92

I went over the edge finally. I actually blocked down, and went crazy. I couldn't see then when I could see I thought I saw things crawling everywhere. Then I got a weird sensation and totally freaked I almost screamed but I knew if I did I would be in trouble. BIG TROUBLE! So I didn't. I don't know how I knew how not to scream but it was really freaky!! I didn't know what was happening. Everything is just happening to fast for me. I have so much to worry about. My grades, my life, my friends. Flute (band) I'm just so scared everything is happening so fast. I am just having a lot of trouble coping. I have a lot of problems; everyone seems to think MARTI miss stable and secure, Marti when I'm not so stable and secure after all I'm really the one here with problems, I am so MESSED UP!!

My life stinks; I just got grounded for not cleaning the kitchen. I'm confined to the house till further notice - I need help but I don't know where to turn. GOD PLEASE HELP ME! I don't mean to be a Bitch but I just do I don't know why. Maybe you can tell me? PLEASE! If you can, please tell me, you are my only hope you are my last hope, please you're my best friend please help me. I have got so much on my mind what did I do to deserve this; I need so much help everything is hitting me like a steam locomotion. BAMB Right where it hurts, right in the HEART!!!!!!!

HELP!!! PLEASE!!!!!!

(There is a picture of a child crying in the diary at this point, it is a little girl with tears like rain running down the page and next to it says). (ME!!) Meaning Marti. :(:(:(

Then it continues: Depressing!! I need someone to talk to. Please help Me! I'm crying out for help but everyone has forgotten Me!! Marti Dudley

For field trip,

Tomorrow, Tuesday December 15, 1992 to see holiday memories. Money for gift shop at stage west. Don't forget pocket book and receipt to go on the field trip. Don't forget after school band concert. Ask mom if she baked. Ask her if she can go early so I can pass out programs and so she can set up. Write a note to Ronnie. Bring progress reports to school, for Miss Pall, Mr. Roberts, and Mrs. White. Write in diary. Ask mom if dad has school, tell mom I paid Jan. Tell her I AM going to the dance. Ask her what my punishment REALLY is since I don't know. My father is a JERK. I hate him you know all I wanted to do yesterday was KILL HIM. I HATE him A LOT. I am so messed up. Especially in the head. I don't know whether or not I coming or going it's awful absolutely awful!!!!!

Father's day

This is your day

Your only day

A day to enjoy

A day to relax

To think about what

The day does mean

What, does the day mean?

It means.........

Without me, there wouldn't

Be Father's Day, So...

Feel lucky to have me around,

Always remember without me.....

You wouldn't have a day to,

Be Lazy!

Marti

The children still loved their father even though he was an abusive monster. They still had hopes and dreams that someday things would be good for all of us. Through her words, Marti tried to tell her father how special she and her brother were. But of course he didn't listen and didn't hear her cries for help.

Marti,

How's my girl this afternoon? Mommy feels yucky. Daddy called to say sorry for not giving me a kiss. He also asked if you were okay. See he does love us. We just have to look past the anger, even though it is hard to do. Something must have happened at work yesterday. I asked if he was better and what happened. He said it was a long story and didn't tell me. So how was school today? Hope you held up okay with the children making fun of you cause of your voice. If you feeling better talking to me by writing notes to me that is okay. But I do hope we can talk face to face also. Well got to go my arm is falling off.

I LOVE YOU

MOMMY

☺

Don't worry be happy.

February 10, 1994

It's been over a year since I've written. It seems almost like an eternity. It seems like I only come to you when I need help. Well guess what, I need help again. I am in desperate need of help! NOBODY to turn to, nowhere to go! My dad is beginning to complain again about his walls closing in on him. Before we all know it he'll want a divorce. You know something? I want to hell out of this house, to hell out of this town, to hell out of this state and to hell out of this country! I want to Hell out of my life! I desperately need help again and here I am! Now dad thinks I'm on drugs, because my mom ratted on me to my dad, cuz I was talking crazy. Well excuse me if I've got a little more than a problem. My dad is so Fucking STUDPID! I HATE HIM! HATE HIM! HATE HIM WITH A PASSION! I DESPISE HIM! I HOPE WHEN HE DIES HE BURNS IN HELL FOR ALL OF ETERNITY AND MORE!

I'm fucked up in the head, I'm afraid of everything now my dad and mom both are telling me it's all my fault. Then turning around and saying I can trust them and that they are always there for me. You know what. Bull Shit. That's nothing but a crock! God knows I need help, but does anyone want to help, No, GOD No! Help Marti that would be a capital sin, it would deserve capital punishment, for heaven sakes, it would earn the death penalty. For God sakes someone could even be beheaded for helping me! Aw Hell! What a world. Life Sucks, Life is a Bitch then you die! My father is a Fucking Asshole. Mom doesn't even know what the hell she is doing, or whatever the hell she is saying. She'll say or do anything to please ANYONE! My brother is even a different story. I've got to go; I'll never hear the end of this if I get caught doing this instead of doing my homework. I'll definitely write more later. See ya later. Love ya Marti Dudley.

I NEED HELP DESPERATELY HELP ME!

This was the last entry my daughter made in her diary. We did write notes to each other, which you will read throughout this book. Here she was desperately calling out for help and I could do nothing to help her. We were all trapped in a world of complete misery, abuse and turmoil by the hand of the man (my husband, and their father) who was supposed to love, care and shelter us, but never did.

To Marti

I'm sorry I have not been very understanding lately. I understand you are going through a lot and I'm sorry I overlooked you. You gave me a lot to think about today. We have been giving Victor a lot of attention, because he has had it hard. But you always did so well and we forget that you still need help once in a while too. We've all been on edge because of daddy lately. I had a talk with him last night. I asked him if he wants out of this marriage. He said NO. He just has a lot to deal with. We have to try and pull together like when daddy was away. We got along so well. This gift (necklace) is not a bribe. It is just to say I love you and I am sorry.

Love Mommy

I mentioned about Tim being away in this note. He was in the service and went away a lot for work. The children and I had really great times when he was away. There was no pressure, no being afraid at 4:30 when he walked in the door, no shaking because we didn't know what was coming. We laughed, played and had fun. We had what we wanted for meals, pancakes, English muffin pizza, homemade sandwiches or whatever we could think of that was fun. All the things the children liked to have. I would make a smorgasbord board and put out what they asked for. With smiling faces and eager little fingers they would make up their own plates. Supper was always at the kitchen table but when Tim was away I would put a blanket down on the floor in the family room. We would have a picnic inside while watching a fun movie. It was usually a Disney movie. Our favorite was Chitty Chitty Bang Bang. We could do whatever we wanted and not be afraid to breathe or look the wrong way or feel like we were walking on eggshells. Victor didn't have to worry about getting hit every day for nothing. Marti didn't have to worry about getting poked in the chest and I could relax and enjoy my children without being a blocker or protector. The more he went away the more we enjoyed it. We really had something to look forward to whenever he told us he was going away. Sometimes it was actually hard for me to contain my excitement about him going away. If he knew how I felt he would have made life more of a living hell than it already was.

Mom,

He is gonna catch me writing this - you didn't give me a bad life. He did. You gave me life he didn't give me life! If he wasn't such a PRICK! We would all be happier!

Got to go,

Love ya 4ever

Marti

Marti,

I am so sorry for this morning. I never want you to go away and I am sorry I told you to go away and I am sorry I told you to keep going on the bike. I didn't mean it. I have so much to deal with, and when you kept at me, it was my way of not dealing with it. Things are bad now. With you threatening to run away, it only puts more pressure on me. It only says that I am not a good mom. I am sorry for that. I guess with everything going on, I forgot the most important part of my life. And that is, I am a mom. Sorry. I know you are tired of hearing sorry, sorry, but I don't know what else to say or do. I am just as confused as you. I love daddy too and it hurts me that he won't hug me or say he loves me. It hurts that he won't tell you or your brother either. Maybe if you tell him how you feel it will help. I do know that we cannot give up. That will only show we don't care. I know that we do care; otherwise it would not hurt so much if we didn't. So if we want things to get better we have to stick it out no matter how bad it gets. By giving each other strength it will give daddy strength to deal with himself. But if we quit then he won't have anything to fight for and then he won't get better. Right now dad needs our love even if he won't give it back. I know it is not fair and it is hard but together we can do it. You and I have so much love for each other and now we need it more than ever. By you being here for me and letting me write you this helps me so much. Marti you don't realize the strength you give me by coming home and being here for me. It means so much to me. So please don't think about running away anymore. If you want to stay with your grandparents for a while that's fine but don't ever leave me. Okay. I know it seems impossible right now but we will get through this. McTabby was here yesterday and she said God will help us, but we have to help ourselves. So lets you and me make a deal. From now on we will be each other's strength and help each other. I will try to listen to you and give you more time. And be a better mom. And you have to promise not to run away. And even though it will be hard we have to give dad time and space. There is a saying "If you love something set it free." Right now we need to set dad free so he can find himself and then come back to us. We also need to be there for Victor. He is your brother and even though you feel you don't like him, he still needs us. I think you two fight so much because you are not happy and you both also have a lot of anger inside. So the three of us have got to be strong and together we can do it. But, if one of us quits, we get weak. So you see we need us all. Okay. Just remember, none of this is your fault or Victor's. And I don't ever want you to go away. Why don't you write to me? This way you can say whatever you want. And no matter what you write, I won't get mad. You need to express your feelings just like I do. It does help. Okay. And no matter what you write, it won't be wrong because it will be how you feel and letting out your feelings helps. I did it with McTabby yesterday. I yelled and screamed at her. You started this morning by yelling and punching the pillow.

Okay, so write to me.

And always remember.

I LOVE YOU SO VERY MUCH!!!!!!!

MOM

A part of this letter was a farce, my marriage was long over and I knew I didn't love Tim anymore. I was still trying to believe in what was supposed to be. I was still trying to believe in my marriage vows for better or worse and I was still trying to keep my family together. Keep it together, because if I didn't, Tim always told me that he would get the children. I was still trying to talk myself into it as well as give my daughter something to believe in and hope for. I knew he didn't need time and space, that he would not change, but I had to try and believe in it for my children. I really believed that if the children and I stuck together we would be stronger for it. Strength comes in numbers and we still had the three of us. I loved my children with all my heart and knew we could not quit on each other. My children were all I had to hang on to and with my daughter threatening to run away I just could not deal with it. With all the pain, confusion, turmoil and abuse we only had each other to depend on and the children felt that they didn't have me. What good was a mother who was so depressed and who couldn't take care of or protect her children from a monster, their own father? I felt I was trapped in a room surrounded by thick one way mirrors. I could see out but no one could see into my world of devastation. I was slowly descending deeper, misery, despair and depression owned me. There was no way out. The walls were up barricading me from family, friends and the world. The cracks were sealed tight nothing could escape no hope; no cries for help and no love could break through that thick cold glass. No love, no understanding and no compassion could seep into and through those walls either. The life was being sucked out of us; all we could feel, touch and breathe was the icy bitterness that surrounded us.

Marti couldn't keep her word to me, she ran away.

By the time Marti was in her junior year of high school, things were worse than ever before. Marti was grounded, as always, this time for going bungee jumping on a class trip. She called me to tell me about it. She said it was such a thrill to do and was so animated talking about it. Then she begged me not to tell her father. I said I would not, but she would have to when she got home. He would find out somehow. When she got home she showed him the pictures of her jump. He of course got really pissed off at her and grounded her, which we knew was going to happen.

Then he asked her if it was worth it and she said "*yes.*" She got yelled at more for that answer. None of us could even say what was on our mind without getting into trouble for it. If it was not what Tim wanted to hear then it was wrong and we were at fault once more. Looking back I wonder why I insisted she tell him. What a dare devil, so high up just falling through the air, she loved it. Secretly, I was glad she got to do something she truly wanted to do and that she was away from this house so bleak and full of sadness. It wasn't a happy or safe place to be. It wasn't the home I dreamed of having for my family. Marti told me about the band competition, what she and her friends did and about running around at the beach. She had a great time on her trip away from the hellhole, which consumed her every waking breath. I missed her, but was so happy she was out for a while.

The tension in the house was constant, I was always yelling and on edge. Marti and Victor by this time couldn't stand each other and fought all the time. They were constantly screaming at each other, going at each other with fists, name calling, whatever one could do to antagonize the other. It was a particularly bad Friday; Tim came home in an exceptionally foul mood and as typical, things were not to his satisfaction. As hard as we tried we knew that nothing we did was right or good enough for him. Many times we could tell just by the tone of his voice that we had done something wrong; *again.* The first thing out of our mouth would be "what did we do wrong this time?" Marti had been grounded for a month, probably for being on the phone too long. She was a typical teenager. Her moods lately were spiteful and not nice. It was after supper, Victor had gone down to his room, we had a finished cellar and he wanted his room there. Something was wrong but I did not catch on. Marti kept asking if I needed anything at the Mini Mart up the street, a little convenience store about 100 yards down the main road. I kept telling her no. Didn't give it any mind. Both the kids often went for me. I went about cleaning and she went to her room. Once I finished cleaning I went outside to say hi to Mr. D. He was out by the garage talking to Tim. Don't know what made me go back into the house, but I did. I went into Marti's room, but she was not there. What was there was a letter on her bed. ***My worst nightmare had come true. She had run away.***

To whom it may concern.

Mom –

The first thing is that I love you, and I'm not doing this to hurt you. But I know it hurts more to hear me say that. You never did anything wrong.

Victor –

I told you once; I'll be back for you. I promise take it easy it will all be okay! I PROMISE! And this isn't just an empty promise. I won't break it, like all the other promises around here.

Tim –

There are paragraphs on how you have made my life miserable. But I'll say it short and to the point. I hate you, you have put the fear of god into Victor and I and Mom. I won't do it anymore! Those grades aren't yours, you said I had to show you you're A's, well everything isn't yours! We are the most ungrateful, and selfish children around. Right? Well that's what you think. But you are wrong. And you are wrong for many reasons! But you never want to hear it, so I'm not about to start telling you now! You can shove those paintbrushes, because I won't need them. I'm not good-enough to use them. So, Good bye. You told me if I ever left the confines of YOUR house, I could never come back, so good bye.

Marti Lynn

P.S. I don't know why God put a good person like me in a place like this.

My children were everything to me. The thought of her being out there by herself absolutely terrified me. I ran outside and shoved the letter at Tim ranting endlessly that she was gone and it was his fault. He said Marti was just acting up and he went inside and watched TV. Mr. D went home to let Mrs. D. know Marti had taken off. The first thing I thought was to call her boyfriend but I didn't know his number. I went to his house, which was right down the street from us. I told his mother what happened. She let me know where he was, but she couldn't find the phone number. I was frantic my little girl, my precious child was gone. I went back home pleaded, begged and cried for Tim to help, he said "*Hell No, she wants to act this way tough.*" So I left to track down my daughter. When I arrived, the boys were out working on a car, but they were nervous and jittery. I laid into John. ***Where is she?*** He tried saying he didn't know, but I could tell by his jumpiness that he was lying. Then the man of the house came out and said he better tell me because John's mother had called and warned him of the situation. She found John's friend's phone number after I left and she called thinking she was helping; not knowing Marti would bolt before I got there. When the kids heard the phone ring, Marti high tailed it into the woods. I was shaking so hard my body felt like there was tremors running through it, when I screamed at John to go get her. He told me Marti said she was not going back home. He said Marti told him that she was fed up and sick and tired of all the crap continuously going on in that house. My hands were trembling and I was crying, but I told him okay. I would not force her to come home. I would talk to her grandparents (Mr. and Mrs. D.) to see if she could stay there.

He took off into the woods and I went to the in-laws. They were waiting to hear from me, nervous and concerned. My eyes were burning and the tears kept running down my face. I told them what was going on and they agreed that Marti could come to their house. We all knew the hell it would be if she went home now. The mood Tim was in was fierce and his temper would be unmanageable. Again, one of us had disrupted his day and made things worse for him.

He had absolutely no idea and took no responsibility for Marti running away. I sat in my house, just praying that she was okay and that things would be alright. Crying and hoping. It seemed it was all I could do. The whole time my stomach was in a knot, pacing back and forth with tears streaming down my face Tim just sat watching TV. The in-laws called me later that night to let me know Marti was there. She was hysterical with fear and dread of what was to come. They calmed her down and put her to bed. I could breathe now; at least I knew she was safe for the night. The next morning early I went over to see my daughter. She was still sleeping so I went in and sat quietly on the bed. She woke right up, like me; she had not slept well that night. Marti told me she was tired of the yelling and screaming all the time. She was tired of Victor getting hit all the time and her getting poked in the chest. She said, "You know mom that really hurts." I told her I knew but I couldn't call the police or they would take her and Victor away from me and I would go to jail. All the stuff Tim had drilled into my head. I wasn't good at anything and I couldn't survive without him. I was stuck and couldn't do a damn thing about it and now my daughter was desperately crying out for help. I was ashamed and felt useless. I couldn't fix it. Mom's are supposed to be able to fix everything and I couldn't, so there you have it I was useless and a terrible mom. Over and over again, everything was always my fault; I was no good, he would take my children from me and I'd be out on my own. I couldn't make it without him. I had so little self-esteem at this point, I believed it all. I was scared to death. What was I to do but reassure my daughter that I would try to protect her as best I could. Marti then told me another reason she ran away. That she wanted to see if her father really cared about her. She had to know, and now she truly knew that he did not. She was totally crushed. During this whole traumatic ordeal, he didn't raise a finger, make a call, get up off his chair, ask one question about Marti or even console me. Marti was so upset she kept saying she would run again and that she didn't want to go home. She was terrified. I was so afraid she would run again, I couldn't lose my daughter, my sunshine, my little pumpkin. I talked to Mr. and Mrs. D. and we agreed Marti would stay with them for a few days. This way her father would be cooled off by the time she got home. I went to see her every day. I was so terrified she would bolt again. She had every right to. She knew what was coming when she walked through the steel-like doors of his domain. When Marti did come home, a lecture was waiting (of course) - Tim demanded to know how she *dare* put her mother through this ordeal and informed her that she was a very ungrateful person. Naturally, it ended with her being grounded indefinitely. So the doors were slammed and locked and the bars went up. Marti had no rights at all. Essentially she felt like she was in prison with her dad who had been the judge and jury and now being the warden and guard all rolled into one. He never said if he was upset or worried. He was so absorbed in his own need to control; all he cared about was how much she had embarrassed him.

A week later we left for North Carolina for vacation. The tension was still very high and Tim took every chance he could to make Marti feel bad by needling her ruthlessly, reminding her of her terrible behavior. It's your entire fault we are so on edge, if you weren't so selfish we'd be having a good time. But no you had to act up, so now we are all paying for it. His Jekyll and Hyde was around big time those two weeks. One minute he would be at her, putting her down, scolding her or being nasty to her. Next he would be having a good time at the amusement park with us. We endured going in and out of darkness for two weeks. At the end of two weeks, we got back home to our world of misery. I love my children, but I could do nothing to help. Here my daughter was again crying out so desperately for help and I was just as helpless to do anything for her.

I remember Tim's face, he was stone cold, could care less, I was crying and pleading with him and he just went inside and watched television. I believe that he didn't have control over this and he didn't like it one bit, especially since his father was going to help us. Marti mentioned her grades. Lots of students in high school have a hard time adjusting to a new school and with classes. Marti was no different when she entered high school. She was having a little bit of trouble adjusting to the new environment and the new demands of high school. She was a very good student, mostly A's and some B's. She brought home her first report card for the new school year and had a C on it. Tim hit the roof. This is not acceptable I demand better than this. He talked as if the grades were his grades and even said something to the effect that you are my daughter and those are my grades and you better improve drastically. We couldn't believe it. He even wanted to control her grades, as if they were actually his. He had not yet learned that screaming at her and demanding better of her would not work. The opposite happened. She gave up and said to heck with it. She went into high school wanting to be valedictorian, but when she left she just graduated like all the other students. Marti wasn't a valedictorian and she didn't care.

I've mentioned that my children hated each other and that is clearly the appearance they gave to everyone. They called each other names, kicked each other, slugged each other, pushed, and scratched each other. I now understand that it was their way of coping with their brutal existence. Victor got all the attention even though it was negative and harsh, and Marti felt alone unloved and left out. Not knowing what to do about their miserable lives, they were blaming each other. I was so touched when I read Marti's note to Victor. I knew there was hope, I just didn't know where. The paintbrushes she talks about were from her father. He took art classes and she took art classes, so he decided she should have them. Anything he did for them always had a price, so the brushes didn't mean anything to her. The brushes were just something he gave her so she could do better work for him. With this ordeal behind us we continued to live in our secret abusive world. Hiding and praying for an answer to come, but it evaded us. Not until years later, when I finally found my backbone, and was able to stand up for myself and my children.

14. Victor's Fault

I joined a bowling league with my mother – in – law. Tim insisted that we spend time together. She and I got along pretty well for the most part, but she, like her son, liked things to go her way. On this one particular night, I bowled absolutely terribly. Although I am right handed, it was extremely difficult trying to steady a 12 - pound bowling ball with a much bruised left arm. Every-time I picked up the ball to throw it down the alley it hurt like hell. My mother-in-law didn't know about my arm until we were on the way home. She has a habit of talking with her hands during a conversation, and in doing so, she touched my arm. I flinched in pain, tears ran down my face. She gave me a questioning look. My voice cracked as I then told her what had happened. I showed her a bruise on my arm that was the size of a softball. The largest, blackest and purple bruise I'd ever seen was on my arm. The purple was so dark that it was black as midnight. Not only was my arm bruised, but I could barely move it because of the tremendous amount of pain and swelling. I had wished I could have canceled out that night, but Tim would not have approved of that decision! Mrs. D was shocked. Despair and sadness showed on her face as she listened to what had happened. The night before, after supper, Tim and the children were fooling around on the couch. Tim pinned Victor's arm behind him and wouldn't let go. He was trying to make our son fight to pull his arm out. He always called Victor a wimp and would try to make him wrestle or fight him. Victor didn't want to fight; he was not one for violence. He was a quiet child who, most of the time, played by himself. Victor started to cry. He said his arm was hurting and he couldn't pull it out, "because Daddy has it too tight and he is so big." I could see the hurt on his little face and the panic starting to set in. We both knew he was going to get hurt again. Even with Victor crying and my pleading, Tim still wouldn't let him go. I was getting upset and didn't want to see my son get hurt. I kept begging Tim to let him go. Tim finally let go after a few more minutes of extensive pleading, but not without first pushing hard on Victor's arm making him cry out in pain and, then, brutally shoving him to the floor. He then bellowed at "the wimp" to go to his room.

Tim then proceeded to scream and rant at me, telling me not to open my mouth in front of the kids again. He said that if I had something to say to him, I'd better do it in the privacy of our bedroom so he would not be embarrassed. Again, Tim stated that I better not ever ridicule him in front of the kids or anyone else. But, yet, here he was doing the identical thing to me. Then he told me to shut up and that he was going in to deal with Victor. He said he was going to teach him a lesson and how to fight. I followed him into the room because I knew the pain and anguish that he would bestow on our son. Victor was in for a brutal reprimand; I felt it and knew it in my soul. I didn't want Victor hurt again. Tim shoved him onto the bed so hard that he almost bounced off the end of it. Red faced, gritted teeth, and pierced lips he started screaming at Victor informing him he was nothing but a "baby" and a "mama's boy" and a "wimp", and that he needed to learn to fight for himself. All of a sudden Tim went at Victor with swift rapid-fire fist. At the top of my lungs, I screamed at him to stop. But he continued to inflict pain on Victor and the look on my son's face at that moment will forever be embedded in my memory. The fear, bewilderment, anguish and pain were all there. Tim was like a mad man flailing away, not caring that he was pounding uncontrollably on his five year old son. Doing the only thing I felt was possible to protect my son; I jumped on top of him. My son under me, crying and shaking all the while, Tim kept coming down with his fist striking over and over again. Beating and slamming into my arms, my head and back with such brute force. I didn't care; I had to protect my son. I could take it, I was bigger, but a little child could not. Covering my son until Tim finished, knowing that the beating that was just dealt to me, would have landed my treasured little child in the hospital. I look back now, years later as I watch my son, holding his own new-born son; and I realize the tremendous fear that I had. Otherwise I would surely have called the police that night. Once Tim finished, I got up just staring at him in disbelief, tears running down my face. Tim was just standing there, his face tense hands still clinched tight in fist at his side; then he went to Victor and hit him again in the head, and said that was for opening my mouth and butting in again.

Each time I would "interfered" with his abusiveness toward the children, they would be hurt even worse. But I *wasn't* interfering; I was *intervening* on my children's behalf. He couldn't see that I was trying to protect them. All he saw was that I stepped on his toes, and he didn't like it. As the years went by, I continued to intervene and each time the children got hit once more because I interfered with their father's type of justice. Each time I intervened for my children my heart would race and I felt the pounding throughout my body. I didn't know what was next or what would happen once I stepped in. But, I had to, I couldn't let him just beat them whenever he felt the need to do so. All I could do was keep trying to protect them, in my own way. All I had, and all I knew how to do, was try to protect my children. I wanted out for my children and myself, but was so afraid of Tim because of his many put-downs. The children would say, "Why don't you leave him, Mom?" I couldn't. He made it clear to me that he would have the children, the house, and everything. I knew I wouldn't leave my children with him and I knew they needed a roof over their heads. Tim was still in a volatile mood when he went into the family room to watch TV. I had to make sure the children were okay and out of harm's way for the night, especially Victor. Amazingly, he didn't have a mark on him, though his arm was sore. Marti had either run to her room or was standing frozen to her spot as she watched the ordeal take place. They were put to bed and then I went into the bathroom to check myself. The pain was dreadful. I had a bruise on my back and one on my arm the size of a softball. When I showed it to him he looked at me with his cold eyes and said that I deserved it!

After telling his mother what happened, she was livid. She said she would go home and talk to Tim's dad. The day after I told her the story, his father came over and tried to talk to him, but all Tim did was tell him to butt out and mind his own fucking business. Astonishingly, he said he didn't know what the hell his father was talking about. He was, and is, a very sick individual. **Dumbfounded,** I looked at him and wondered how he could not know what he had done to us just the night before. So vivid in our minds the yelling, screaming, crying, fists pounding finding their mark each and every time. The pain, the children still so afraid of him and my arm swollen; and with each movement I made, there was excruciating pain. So, this was how he would get away with his fits. He said he had a "black out" and didn't remember a thing that happened the previous night. Tim said he had absolutely no idea what we were talking about or how I got the bruises. He also had no idea why the children shook every time he approached them and why they didn't want to be around him. Now was a new excuse for him to not take responsibility for his atrocious behavior and actions. How convenient for him.

Although his parents were demanding, especially at the holidays, they were there for the children. I was so terrified Tim would take the children away that I only told them part of what went on in our house of terror. Many times they tried talking to Tim, but he would just blow them off. They knew we got screamed at, belittled and put down each day; and they knew Victor got hit every day and on occasion Marti too! Marti usually was quiet, she was so afraid. Most of the time after these incidents Tim would start yelling at her and poke her hard in the chest telling her she'd better not get like her brother, or she would also pay the consequences. But of course, Tim never remembered these occurrences, because he would declare that he had another blackout. Many times his mother said she would take Victor to live with her, so he wouldn't get hit. Victor was about eleven or twelve years old when we finally decided to send him to live with his grandparents. Things were unquestionably bad and we were afraid Victor would be killed one day. Victor at this time just didn't seem to care. No matter what he did it was wrong. He would get belted or screamed at and grounded every day. His life was a "no-win situation." Life began to lose meaning. My children would probably hold the world's record for being grounded the most in their lives. They wouldn't get grounded for just a night or a week but for weeks and months at a time. This, needless to say, caused them to become more rebellious.

The four of us, Tim, his parents and I agreed that Victor would stay with them for a while. Tim felt his father could "straighten out" Victor. He truly believed he had nothing to do with why Victor was acting up all the time. Victor didn't want to go. He promised to be good and not cause any more trouble. He believed it was his entire fault, because his father drilled it into his head time and again. Now he was pleading with us to stay home, promising he would be better and he wouldn't cause the family to be mad all the time. He felt that we didn't love him anymore and that we just wanted to get rid of him. It is unbelievable to me today to recognize the pain this child was in and how inept we all were in helping him because we stood behind the barrier of fear. Yes, I wanted him gone but not because I wanted to get rid of him. I knew that if he were out of the house he would not be brutalized all the time, threatened or screamed at. Victor stayed over the in-laws about two months, everyday begging to come home. He promised to be good and said he was sorry for causing trouble. I couldn't make him understand that it wasn't his fault. It was for his own good, but he couldn't see that because his father drilled it into his head, how bad he was, and that he couldn't do anything right. So, of course, now, he thought it was because he was no good and a bad boy. Victor said we were his family and he wanted to be with us, he just didn't care how bad it was, he just wanted a family to love him. Nothing was ever Tim's fault; there was always someone else to blame. So, no matter how much we told Victor, it wasn't his fault it didn't matter. He took the weight of all the problems on his own shoulders, and his father let him. After a period of about two months we came up with a plan that we thought would help Victor come home. We sat the children down and set up Tim's rules and regulations for them to follow. At this time, Tim agreed to back off some, but said the kids should "know their place." Tim said he came first, no matter what the situation; the children and I were always last. In my opinion, I thought the children should have come first. But trying to make it so, only infuriated Tim and made things worse. He didn't agree, always Tim first, never anyone else. He would never listen to us and if he did we were always wrong and he was always right.

It often felt like we were in boot camp. Many times I'd be going around like a mad woman getting things done to help the children. After school they had to come straight home, do their homework and chores. If they had anytime left, they could go outside to play before supper. Things were okay for a little while but that black hole hovered over us all the same waiting to swallow us up again. After a while, Tim came up with the idea of sending Victor to military school. I really thought it would help him, plus it would get him out of our wretched house. I knew school would be strict, but I also knew Victor wouldn't get belted around and abused at school. It turned out to be much too expensive for us, but that didn't stop Tim from threatening our son with it all the time. "You better behave, or we will send you away and you will not see us for a long time, not even for holidays. "

Victor was mad at the world and took it out on me. He hollered at me all the time and never did what was asked of him. His verbal abuse was non-stop, and many times he told me how much he hated me. It always hurt and it would break my heart when he said that to me. The only way for me to have the slightest leverage, was to threaten him about being sent to military school, which I hated to do. I felt it made me no better than Tim! Victor knew it was an idle threat from me so that stopped working after a short while.

In anger, I once told Victor that I wished he had never been born. Not because I didn't love him, or want him; but because he would not be going through a life of hell, so unfairly given to him. I have always regretted saying that to my precious son.

15. Vehicles and Toys

Marti was about ten months old and we were on our way to Massachusetts from Michigan, where we planned to visit for a long weekend. The trip usually took about five hours. We were sitting in the cab of the truck, Tim was driving, Marti was in her car seat in the middle and I was sitting in the passenger's seat. Five hours is a long time for an adult to sit still never mind a ten-month-old baby. Marti started to fidget and her foot hit the shifter. Yes, I understand it could have been moved and caused an accident, but what Tim did was uncalled for and shocked me. He slapped Marti's bare leg so hard that it left a very large red hand print. Of course she started to scream and big tears slid down her face. Tim kept hollering at me to shut her up and keep her legs over where they belonged. I tried explaining that Marti was only a little baby and didn't kick the shifter on purpose. He didn't want to hear it. He again continued yelling at me to shut her up and keep her legs where they belonged. It was not possible to shut a baby up when she had her leg smacked as hard as she did. The rest of the ride was very long. Marti finally stopped crying but her little body shook with every sobbing breath she took. I kept my hands around her legs to keep them away from the shifter in order to protect her from another unwarranted smack. It was just the beginning of our weekend and now I dreaded the rest of our trip to Massachusetts, not to mention the drive back to Michigan. I think that is when I really started to hate that truck. It was a black 1971 Ford pickup. Tim had always wanted that truck and his father never let him drive it when he was younger. When we got married his father sold it to Tim for $500.00. Years later Tim's father said if he had known the trouble the truck would cause he never would have sold it to Tim. The truck was terrible on gas and uncomfortable to ride in, it was also a standard, which I could not drive. I found it amazing that his father would think it was the truck that was the problem!

Money was always tight for us, but Tim always found money to sink into the truck. He would borrow money to put new mag wheels on it, or a new tail pipe, or headers for it. Often I would get money for my birthday or holidays. I would use it on the children or to help pay bills. Something that was necessary. Not Tim, any extra money went into the truck. Paint job, fixing little dings and constant wax jobs. When we moved into the house our budget was really tight, but Tim had to get the rust fixed on the truck. He took it to the garage and ordered the work done. Not just a little spot, but a costly project. The mechanics were to take the cab and the bed off the frame. Sand down and fix anything and everything that was rusting then repaint it. It cost over $2000.00 to have it done. All this time I was juggling bills around to keep up with them and keep our heads above water. Tim had to have all the latest and greatest things for the truck. A new canvas cover with support bars and straps to snap on the truck. New engine parts, seat and steering wheel covers. He had a number of different caps for it because he was never satisfied with the one he had at the time. He would get tired of the cap and put the cover on it. Get tired of the cover and want the cap back on it. I often wished he cared that much about us! Each time the children and I would have to lift the cap on or off the bed of the truck using 2x4 that he set underneath it. We had to each take a corner of a 2x4 and lift the cap off the truck bed and carry it around to the back yard and place it on the sawhorses set up for it. Or we had to heave the cap off the horses and haul it out front to the truck. The children and I absolutely dreaded this. It was a daunting task and was met with trepidation. We knew if we dropped the cap or scratched the truck we might as well be dead. All hell would break out and the abuse would be unreasonable and savagely doled out. We got screamed at many times for not lifting properly, while for us, it was difficult and straining. We were called "stupid" or worse for not being careful or for not wanting to do this, one little thing for him right. Each time, it was the same thing. On and off again, we hated it. One of our neighbors would come over to help us. He felt bad for us and knew the cap was too heavy for us; it weighed at least 300 pounds. Tim decided the truck was to go into antique shows, but it had to be original. Now, more money into the truck, restoring all the hubcaps, fenders, motors parts and whatever he felt needed to be changed. Once or twice a week in the summers, off to antique car shows we would go. Victor did like the car shows. He liked anything his father did, just to get his approval and to be able to spend time with him. Marti and I would rather have stayed home, but we were told we had to go. The truck had to stay in the garage. Heaven help us all if snow or rain got on the precious truck. Victor would take the trash out to the street through the garage. One day, Victor hit the truck with a trash barrel! I thought Tim would kill him that day. He kept screaming at him for being so, "stupid and clumsy", and asking how could he do that to his father? Then telling us over and over about all the hard work he put into the truck. Big deal, it was only a material thing. But that is the way Tim was, his possessions were more important to him than his family. Victor didn't realize he had even scratched the truck. Tim just kept hitting him until he said he did it. After Victor admitted to what his father was demanding, Tim stopped hitting him. Tim got what he wanted, his son to once again bow down to his will. After that Victor would agree that he did things wrong, even when he didn't just so he would get the beating over with. Victor said he would get hit once if he agreed right away instead of getting hit five or six times if he didn't admit to his error immediately. I asked Victor if he was okay and he said," it just doesn't matter anymore and it doesn't hurt anymore anyway." He was so used to getting hit and put down, that he was hardened to it and said he didn't feel it. He also said he would hit his kid upside the head when he got older. Sad, but that is what he knew.

Tim was supposed to give the truck to Victor when he turned 21; it was in our divorce agreement. But Victor went off to college and didn't want the truck, so his father gave him the 1991 red truck instead. Victor said he didn't want the black truck. Even at 21 years old he was in some way still afraid. If he did anything to the precious truck, he would never hear the end of it. I too had fear inside me if I damaged the black truck. With the truck taking up one side of the garage I had to pull the car in as far away from the truck as possible. The Dodge wagon was wide and long. I had to pull in at an angle and then straighten out as the car cleared the doors. The car was over past the doorway by at least a foot. Backing out was just as tricky because now I had to go out at the same angle that the car was pulled in at. Life was full of fun for me! One day, I didn't turn the wheels enough and I hit the garage door hard. The bumper on the car was very strong so it pulled the frame out of place by at least six inches. Oh God, I knew I was going to be in a tremendous amount of trouble. Instantly, sweat poured down my back and my head pounded as if there was a drummer inside it. In a panic, I called my brother in-law, asking him to come over and fix the door. He came directly over and pounded the door back into place for me knowing full well that Tim would explode if he saw what happened to the garage. Tim never knew what happened that time, because the frame was in place and, luckily for me, the car had no damage. Always being in a state of fear, I should have known that there would be a next time. When I hit the door again, it could not be hidden from him. The same thing happened. I didn't turn the wheels enough and took out the frame to the door. This time wood splintered and went flying into the air landing across the road. Thank goodness there was no damage to the car and no one was hurt by the flying debris. Tim was extremely angry with me for damaging the garage door. I was screamed at, yelled at, and repeatedly told that I was stupid. I was reminded again and again that I put the car away many times and should have paid better attention to what I was doing. Now, he had to take time out of his day to fix the garage door. I did feel stupid and couldn't understand then, as I do now, how I could have made the same mistake again. When I lived in fear, always rushing to be sure everything was perfect so I could derail the next outburst; it is easy to understand how this happened again. What is not so easy to understand is how, living in that state, I didn't get killed in a fatal accident.

Yes another truck, a red one this time. An automatic, that was good for me. I told Tim I needed to be able to drive the truck in case of an emergency. We had four vehicles a 1985 Dodge wagon, 1971 Ford truck, 1991 Ford truck and a 1993 Chevy Malibu. Why we needed four vehicles, I don't know. But every year it was a different one until he was able to upgrade to a better one. We had a Cadillac, two Broncos, Mustang and more that I don't remember. Tim put money into them thinking he would make a profit, but he never actually made a profit on any of the vehicles he bought. We couldn't even register the Taurus as it turned out to be a stolen car! We had to get that all straightened out, but still he would sell it and buy another car. And, then we moved into what I call the toy phase.

The toys started showing up. And each time he said it was because I wanted it. A pop-up camper was bought. I never cut the grass, but the riding lawnmower was next to appear, which he said was for me. And then the boat showed up. It was some old thing a friend at work had. Tim didn't talk about it with me or mention he was thinking about a boat. The guy just showed up one day and dropped it off in the driveway. Oh, didn't you know? Tim bought it from me for $300.00? WHAT! What a piece of junk. It got the name Tow Boat, because every time we went out on it we had to get towed back to the dock. It couldn't even pull one child on a tube, the motor was so slow. His father had a boat and sold it to his daughter and her husband. Tim had wanted that boat for years. When Tim's sister was selling it, I told them not to let Tim know about it. We didn't need it and couldn't afford it. Meg and Ted were having a tag sale and had a "For Sale" sign on the boat. And don't you know, Tim decides to go visit that day. *Knowing* full well I didn't want it they sold it to him anyway. They had no choice. Tim was adamant about the boat and once he wanted something, there was nothing anyone could say to change his mind. And, of course, he came home with the boat.

The children and I had everything, yet we had nothing. Big house, four vehicles, boat, camper, riding lawn mower, clothes, food, paid bills, pool, brand new storage shed, celebrated birthdays and holidays, but it was nothing. We were not happy, we cried all the time, felt like we were walking on eggshells constantly and went through each day in fear with that never ending cloud of anxiety hanging over our heads. I could see the fear in my kid's eyes and hear the quiver in their voices, but I could not do a thing about it. I was in a paralyzed state by his treatment to us. I was empty, just a shell that looked like a normal person, but I was far from a normal person. My heart ached, my life was out of control and I felt helpless to deal with any of it.

16. My Personal Pain

My sister could be very stubborn at times. When she was mad at her husband, often she wouldn't talk to him for a few days or he was given a nasty attitude. Tim always threw that in my face. He was such a hypocrite. He would say, "It is a good thing you are not like your sister, because if you were you would be out of here so fast you wouldn't know what hit you." But, it was always okay for him to have an attitude with me or not to talk to me. He would go a day or more, sometimes a week without speaking to me. There was clearly a double standard.

I woke to another dreary day. The sky was dark with threatening rain clouds, another day of rain pouring down deepening my depression, matching the misery and gloom lurking over my head. Each day the same miserable gray darkness inside and out consuming me with each breath I took. Not knowing when the storm would hit and not knowing to what severity it would unleash upon me.

And so it began. I would hurt myself to get his attention and because I felt so bad about myself I felt I deserved it. *I didn't care anymore.* I was no good and deserved to be punished for not being a good wife and mother. I truly believed this. I was that depressed and as the result I became very irrational in my thinking. *I became a cutter.* The first time I inflicted pain to myself was in the shower. I was crying after another put down, feeling really low and distressed knowing I couldn't do a thing about it. Had the razor in my hand and just kept looking at it. It mesmerized me. The sharp two edges all shiny and bright. I took the razor and slid it up the back of my right leg. I watched the blood run down the calf of my leg and pool into the tub. I cut it about six inches long, but not deep. It stung a little, but not much. I was dead inside, so I couldn't feel much. I wrapped myself in a towel; put a rag on the cut. Then I went in to show Tim the long slice on my leg. It got a little attention for about a minute. What did you do? Be more careful. Wow Wee! It took several band-aids to cover it up. Every now and then the razor would slip in the shower. I got attention from others, but not from Tim.

The night before Tim was to go away for work we had a huge fight over sex. As usual he yelled and I would cower just like always. He went away for a week and didn't call once, his way to punish me again. This time I took a straight edge razor numbed the side of my left foot and cut deep. My foot hung over the sink with the blood pouring out of the gaping cut about an inch long and deep. I shook as I watched the blood, bright red, swirl into the drain. This was going to need stitches it wasn't going to stop bleeding on its own. This time it hurt some but not bad because I had numbed the area first. Infection possible, no I had sterilized the razor. I was so down and in need of some attention, love and a hug. Sick, here I numbed my foot and sterilized the razor to protect myself from hurt but I had to hurt because of all the hurting. Hurting got attention that's what we all knew and knew it well. I wrapped a towel around my foot and called my best friend, Moe. He took me to the hospital. I got six stitches in the side of my foot. He stayed with me late that night making sure I was okay He helped with dinner and the children too. He was always there for us no matter what. I tried to call Tim later but had to leave a message. He never returned the call. He was being so pig headed and spiteful. I went the whole week with stitches in my now swollen foot, limping and he didn't know. By his actions he showed that he didn't care. When Tim got home, he didn't say much. He just said he was mad at me and had a right to be; that he needed time away from us. Tim said that it was *his way* of *punishing me* and *getting back at me*. The darkness continuing to close in on me is what I felt when he got home. What did I cut my foot on he asked? I told him a razor sticking out of a box down cellar. I was always bare foot. That was the extent of his caring, not a smile; I miss you or a hug.

He was away again and I did the same thing only this time I cut my foot (the same foot) on broken glass down cellar. The blood ran down the drain with the cold water. Again it only smarted a little brainless me always barefoot. He didn't say much. More stitches and another trip to the hospital. We went to a wedding and instead of being concerned about my foot he didn't seem to remember because we danced all night. My foot was so swollen the next day I could hardly walk on it and it throbbed continuously. It was a good thing we had a long drive home from New Jersey, and I could keep my foot up. Another bad day, another put down, another slip with the razor in the shower. This was the sixth or seventh time most likely more. I lost count. I just wanted a little bit of love and attention without it hurting. The pain I caused myself was nothing. What he did certainly was destructive, so I craved his love and kindness and actually believed that somehow he would love me if I was hurt. That was his understanding of love. You always hurt the ones you love. Only with him it was literal.

Another time he wanted to horse around and I didn't want to. I always got hurt, why would I want to? I wanted to be able to keep an eye on the children. But he always had to win. We had words and I was told again, "don't be like your sister, or out you go." Always inferring I would go, but the kids would stay. I went into the bedroom, feeling small and useless as always and I slammed my head into the bedpost a few times. The first hit hurt and after that I didn't notice the pain. I was in pain continuously that this little bit was nothing. Nice goose egg rose up about an inch high, but didn't even bruise. He didn't notice. When I mentioned it, again be careful. Not are you okay? It was always an excuse to admonish me for stupidity or clumsiness rather than an opportunity to show affection. We had another fight before he left for work. Things were continuing to get worse and worse all the time. I took the straight edge razor after numbing my finger on my left hand and jammed it into my finger running it down the length of it. The razor went sideways this time so there was a big flap of skin hanging as well as blood running down my hand into the sink. I figured this time he had to give me attention if I drove to the base in my nightgown and bathrobe with a sliced finger. When I arrived Tim got really irate. All I did was make his bad day even worse.

He grumbled at me and didn't show any love whatsoever, just said that I had inconvenienced him yet again. He didn't even drive me to the ambulatory center. I had to follow him in my own car with my finger sliced and aching. That time I got butterfly stitches. On the way out, I said bye. He just looked at me with a cold emotionless expression and said bye. With tears in my eyes and feeling so lonely, unloved, and desperate, I asked this uncaring man for a hug. I was so pathetic. Even though he put the children and me through constant hell I still needed to be loved and to feel the warmth of a hug. It was of course a hug with absolutely no feeling behind it; it was like hugging a stone cold pillar. Home I went feeling worse than before because I was now just a sore spot in his life. I was no longer a person, but an inconvenience. Now my finger hurt, but what did I care. I certainly deserved it for being such a waste of a human being. So stupid, just like he had told me so many times.

We had been arguing continuously. So, of course, I was feeling no good and worthless once again. With no end to be seen I was suffocating and nauseous in my own house, the perpetual darkness engulfed me. On this day I was baking brownies for dessert. It didn't even register, what I was about to do. I took the pan out of the oven and placed it right on my left arm and let it set there for about 20 seconds. I don't remember it hurting much. I was so depressed that I just didn't care and was so numb from the inside out. I knew I burned my arm severely and put it under cold water for a while. I got a third degree burn and a huge blister on my arm. I finally understood how my son felt on the day he said to me, "Mommy it just doesn't hurt anymore." He said that to me one day after I asked him if he was okay after his father had beaten him brutally. If Tim showed any sign of caring it was miniscule, because I can't recall anything that he said to me about the burn.

Unlike the scars on my foot, which; I don't see much and don't have to live with the memories as to why I got them. The burn mark, however, is about three quarters of an inch long and half inch wide on my arm. It reminds me of the bastard that he was and of what he persistently put the children and me through for so many devastating years. But it also reminds me that we survived the harsh cruelness that we dealt with every waking moment of every dreadful day for nineteen years. Tim was supposed to be my husband, someone to love me and show me kindness. But nothing worked and it was only when he felt like it and of course the most attention I got was in the bedroom. I was so alone. Trapped, cut off from family and friends with nowhere to turn and no one to talk to. The only ray of hope I had was when Moe would come to visit. He would put a smile on our faces and make a life of complete devastation and misery feel a little better for a few sweet moments. Those fleeting minutes would be filled with laughter, smiles and happiness that we all desperately needed and wanted.

"Things better change or I'm leaving," or "I'm feeling boxed in again," "the walls are getting closer" and "there is never enough sex." These are only a few of Tim's favorite things to say using his threats to keep me in line. He had full control over me and knew it. He had belittled and put me down so much that I truly believed I couldn't make it on my own. I was actually feeling threatened to lose him. I would lose the house, the children, everything I worked so hard for. Over and over again, I was so tired of hearing these things. The house isn't clean enough "(or correctly)." "What did you do all day besides sit around?" (I worked forty hours a week and still kept house), "What did you buy that for", but he could get whatever he wanted and whenever he wanted it. "I don't want that for supper cook something else." "If you can't keep the kids in line I will." Things would be okay for a few days after his threat to leave. I would be so scared that he would leave and I would lose my children and everything. We were terrified and walked on eggshells. Then it would start all over again, the insults, abusiveness, emotional threats, whatever he would take pleasure in tormenting us with. Of course I knew that it was my entire fault for not being a good mother and wife and, especially, for not being good enough in the bedroom. I would do anything to please him: the house spotless; the children quiet or in their rooms; and, of course, the dreaded sex in his usual rough and uncaring way. I could have been an object, not a person.

He hurt me and of course if I complained it was my fault. I just didn't want "to expand" as he put it. I felt nothing but disgust and degraded time after time. I knew I was no good at sex and did not want it. Hated it! Isolated and alone I had no one to turn to or talk to. This was my secret alone and it was met with complete fear and pain. No one could know of the heartbreaking demoralizing abuse that took place in the bedroom. He had been talking a lot about wanting anal sex, again, but I continually refused. He introduced cream into the sex relationship. He would call me into the bedroom and order me to put something dirty on. Over the years he had given me a number of dirty slinky little outfits to wear if you could call them that. One had strings going this way and that, that I couldn't figure out how to put it on and another was so small and shear I might as well have had nothing on. There were so many different ones, that I hid them in a basket on the top shelf of my closet way in the back. I was so embarrassed that he had given them to me and was afraid someone would find them. I would be mortified if someone knew what I had to wear for him. I know some women may enjoy this, and I don't pass any judgments. I only know that it is not my cup of tea. He would sit on the bed and watch me get into this skimpy little outfit leering at me with that demonic smile on his face. Trembling and very self-conscious, feeling like a slut, I put on the outfit in front of him. Once in bed he would take out the cream and put an endless amount of it on my hand then force me to lubricate his penis. Once that was done he would put a porn video in the TV set. He would then get behind me and rub his penis against my anus for about 30 to 45 minutes inserting the head then pulling out again. Persistently doing, as he wanted to me. I would squeeze shut as taut as I could and try to move away but he held me to him. Sweat covered my body and muscles cramped as I tried to fight off the pressure of his body. I was in my husband's arms but I was so alone, helpless, feeling unloved, violated and used. How can a person put emotion into lovemaking when you are not making love just being abused? Being used for his personnel playtime and that is all sex was. I didn't want to touch him and surely didn't want him to touch me. The sooner it was over the better. He would get mad at me for just lying there and not touching him. He would ask, "How do you like this" and he would lie there making one motion with his hand on my leg. I didn't say anything; I knew even though he asked and one would think I had a choice, it would be putting myself out there for more physical and verbal abuse if it was not what he wanted to hear. Once he had enough of the porn he would turn me over and finish himself off, get up and get ready to go to sleep. No cuddling no endearments and no love went with his sex. I always went into the bathroom and scoured myself before I would return to what felt like a sadistic sex chamber.

One night we were in the bedroom and, again, he stated that he wanted anal sex. As always, I refused to do it. No way. It was not natural for me, and I knew that it would injure me again, causing severe pain, and just the thought of it sickened me. He decided that night that he wanted it, without regard for anything I had to say. We were laying in bed, him over me. I was *pleading* with him not to, I *didn't* want it and it would hurt. He just kept saying it would be okay. He had this leering look on his face a belligerent look I'd never seen before. His lips were tight in a thin gratifying smile. As he started to turn me over I stiffened up and fought to stay on my back. He used force and turned me over and started rubbing his penis against my rectum. I tried to roll back over, but he applied more force and kept me pinned in that repulsive butt raised position. I was so nervous and scared shaking more violently with each moment that passed. I felt sick to my stomach my whole body trembling. I didn't want this. After a few minutes of his toying with me a little pressure then nothing repeatedly I thought he wasn't going to force himself into me but was still petrified. How brainless of me. My body ached from being so tense, anxieties causing my head to throb in pain and every muscle in my body spasming from fright. My butt hurt from squeezing my muscles tight together to protect myself. There was no way he could enter me. I was so tight and too small and tense beyond belief. There was a brief moment of nothing then all of a sudden without notice of what was to happen he just rammed his penis into me. He **raped** me up the ass. As the searing pain ripped through me, I screamed and started to cry hysterically. My entire body shuddered; tremors of pain ripped through me and hatred filled me as I pleaded with him to stop my voice cracking and barely audible. Tim **please stop**, **get it out** it hurts I'm **begging** you to **stop,** Tim **don't,** you're too big, **please don't,** you're hurting me. In and out the pain seizing me ripping through me with each of his thrusts his hands on my butt holding me captive unable to move. If the children heard me scream, I don't know because they had been *warned* many times never to enter the bedroom no matter what if the door was closed. After what seemed like an eternity of me pleading he finally stopped his unwanted invasion and pulled out. But he had to finish himself. In his irritation with me he flipped me over as if I were a rag doll and entered me in the normal fashion. He was angry with me I could see it in his deep cruel eyes, the tension in his face and the sneer of his thin lips. He finished himself and got up. I was still crying and sobbing. I went into the bathroom with a tear-streaked face. I hurt terribly, couldn't stop crying or shaking. I was devastated, humiliated and torn apart by this mean despicable person. He wasn't my husband but a cruel sadistic sick monster that I was chained to, without hope of ever escaping. I burned with pain; my hands shook violently as I washed myself with warm soapy water. Ever so gently I wiped my now swollen rectum. When I did, I found blood, bright red blood. I knew he had torn my insides up. I was even more traumatized wondering if he had done something to my insides, but who could I tell? No one! I was alone in this insanity. I went back into the bedroom, still shaking and crying and shoved the bloody tissue in his face. He just looked at me and didn't say a word. No words of regret or any emotions to be seen. His face was made of stone.

For a long time I knew I did not love him, but now I knew I *hated* him. I hated him for what he had done to the children and me. I hated the mental and physical beatings he bestowed upon us. I hated his lack of respect for us and now I hated that he made me want to die all the more. I hated sex more and more; I despised it and only feared it now. I did everything to avoid it, never looking forward to time in the abysmal bedroom. As he did his thing, I just lie there and cry it disgusted me to have him touch me. It sickened me to have his hands on me. To have his foul degrading insensitive mouth touch my lips or breast would only make me sick and want to vomit. Every time we had sex I would go into the bathroom to wash his filth off of me and scour my mouth out. What was I to do? So like all the times I was upset after sex, or because of the life I had, I would curl up into a fetal position. I would get as small as was possible, my knees pulled up tight one hand grasping my pillow and the other over my heart and lie there and weep. I didn't want to be near him and I most certainly did not want him to touch me. The further away from him I was the better I felt. I lay there in my little spot at the top edge of the bed distraught and thinking how to die. I could run my car into a tree, maybe off a bridge, maybe even slit my wrists or take a bottle of pills, but always two little voices calling out to me. *Mommy! Mommy!* I knew I could never leave my babies in the hands of this loathsome brute. More self inflicted injuries would occur because the hurt kept hurting and the attention we got was through his abusive ways.

Any dreams of a romantic relationship had long since disappeared. I knew it would never happen, not in my wildest dreams. His destructive ways overshadowed any little good he may have done in the past. Tim would often take the children and me out to dinner, but never just the two of us. Lots of times he would invite his parents to go with us. Not only did it not give us time for us, but he would always pay the bill. He had to play the big shot so when we went out, even if we were invited, he would insist on paying. I often told him not to, because we could not afford it but he just ignored me as always. When we first got married he would buy me a little box of chocolates and get me a card for Valentine's Day, but never flowers. It made me feel special that he took the time to do that for me. It was romantic, because we could not afford much in the beginning of our marriage. But after a few years he just stopped getting me anything. I don't know why, but he just stopped. I believe he just couldn't be bothered to spend a little time getting his lowly wife something. One year we went to visit his aunt and uncle for Valentine's Day weekend. We went shopping and she asked him what he was getting me. When he said "nothing", she got upset and made him get me a gift. It was a cute little animal with a pink hat and fluff around the neck. He made sure to let me know that the only reason he bought it for me, was to shut his aunt up. And of course he would want sex that was his way to be romantic. He thought that sex was romance. Yes, it could be if the circumstances were different, but in our situation it was never right. Love, respect and kindness were missing.

My dreams of a romantic night would be to first get a baby sitter for the children and not invite his parents to go with us. Take a nice hot bath, relaxing to soft music while soaking in billions of rose-scented bubbles. Then, spend time getting dressed up nice and pretty. Hair pulled back with curls draping down my back, delicate earrings and necklace glimmering from ear lobes and neck. Feeling beautiful, I picture myself emerging from the room looking and feeling like I am worth something. He looks at me in awe and hands me a single red rose. Then he would accompany me out of the house and open the car door for me. He would escort me into the restaurant that he had called for reservations. We would have a table by the fire or in a secluded corner with candlelight dancing in the breeze. He would order wine and our meals and then toast us as soft music played. After dinner and dessert, we would go out dancing some place quiet with slowly moving melodious music. Just looking into each other's eyes as we held each other close, maybe a sweet kiss once, and maybe a delicate caress. I know I am loved: I can see the sparkle in his eyes as I gaze into them. After dancing to a few love songs, we would go home. While I get ready for bed, I would wear a nice delicate nightgown, he would pull down the covers to the bed and light a candle and put on soft music. He would take me in his arms and hold me tenderly and ever so lovingly. Talking, holding, feeling the love we have for each other and treasuring the moment we are sharing. Just being in the arms of the person I love and cherish should be enough. He takes my hand and gentle guides me into bed were he snuggles close and wraps me safely and contently in his arms. Then ever so slowing, if both of us wanted to and felt comfortable enough, we would make love. But it should not be just sex. It should be making love, the gentle caresses, the decadent kisses and the love making should be felt ever so tenderly, slow, not hurried fulfilling each other's needs as you want your own filled. In my opinion romance isn't just a one-night stand either. It could be a stroll on the beach, going for a walk, hand in hand, sharing popcorn at the movies or waving at each other across the room. It is a look, touch, a kiss of the moment. Knowing the other person waits for me and gives me that sparkling smile when I enter the room or just gives me a hug as he passes by. The comfort I feel even when we are not together, the thoughts of him as I go through the day, the happiness that overwhelms me just knowing his love is there for me makes love making a beautiful experience. Terms of endearment can give way for romance to blossom. *Pain and sadness fill my heart for shattered dreams, never to happen.*

A person has to feel content and happy with who they are and who they are with and in the life they lead, because just having sex is not the answer to an unhappy situation and to me it is not romantic in the least. But this was not the way with Tim, we never went out just the two of us and if we did he expected sex when we got home. It was his payment for taking me out. Every year we would go the Rhode Island for our anniversary in April. It was always cold and dreary and a few times it snowed. I have to say it was fun sitting in the hot tub with it snowing outside. I asked to go someplace different, but Tim was the kind of person that was stuck. He would only do certain things and that was what he would stick with each and every year. We took the children with us one year and then we started going with a few other couples. One couple, then two, every year the same thing. It was fun having other people around it kept his mind off sex for a little while. But one year he wanted to make a record for having sex. *He* decided we would have sex nine times in a three day period. A place for his deposits that is what I was. By the time we went home I was sore and totally disgusted and fed up with him. He was not a stud and his sex sessions were degrading. Romance, ha, none whatsoever. It was just "wham, bam, thank you, ma'am" to make him feel like a macho man and to prove to himself that he could have orgasms that many times. He was not a stud and his sex sessions were only degrading. His "sex on demand" only made me feel less like having sex with him and more like I was being violated once again. There were no gentle hugs and kisses and no cuddling afterward. There is nothing romantic when a person goes by and roughly sticks his hands up your shirt and pinches your nipples, or goes down your pants without any consideration for you. "We are on number five - only four more to go." Oh, *that* (the number of times you are going to get screwed by the man you cannot stand) is what a person *really* wants to hear all weekend!

Mother's Day was special for me. For this day, I felt that Tim, being the father of the two beautiful children whom I loved with all my heart, should work with the children to plan an enjoyable day for me. I felt that it was his responsibility as their dad. But, as with Valentine's Day, he would get me a little something the first few years, and then, nothing. He said that I was not his mother and that he didn't have to get me a thing. However, he, as their father, *should* have taught them how to honor and show love for their mother. On the other hand, when it came to Father's Day, it was made clear to me that I had the responsibility to make sure that the children and I had something for *him*. His hints were well noted, and I knew what was expected of me and what he expected to receive on that day. I remember that he joined a local club at some point later in our marriage, and because it was "expected" - "the right thing to do," so to speak - he started taking all of us to this club for Mother's Day breakfast. We also went to the club for Father's Day breakfast. We started spending both Mother's Day *and* Father's Day there - with his family. Anyone he could round up for breakfast was invited to join us. When "eyes were watching," Tim would do the "right" thing - but was *that* the intent of these special days? For many years I got handmade items from my children on Mother's Day, which meant more to me than some store-bought thing Tim would have picked up at the last minute. Pictures, flowers, hearts, and lots of love would be in those handmade cards from my children. I cherish these precious gifts from my children and still have some of them. The bottom line is that Tim just didn't get it - *I* was the mother of *his children* and he should have shown me respect by celebrating that fact on this special day - but he did not.

For my birthday, Tim would take the children with him to pick something out for me. My daughter told me that he would have her pick out a card for him. He could not even be bothered to do that. He even told me that he gave his mother money sometimes to buy my birthday or Christmas gifts. He didn't know what to get me and couldn't be bothered to spend a little time, effort and thought on his wife. But, when it came to *his* birthday, he made it clear what he wanted and what I had "better get for him." At Christmas, I had to fill my own stocking because he couldn't be bothered to get me one little thing. I filled it knowing that if it were empty that the children would feel bad. The same went for Easter. I would make everyone baskets, including my own. After a few times of receiving nothing, I made one adult basket for the *both* of us; that is, nothing special for Tim that year. Ironically, on that very day he *did* buy my daughter and me a corsage; but there was a little more to *this* story than meets the eye: Tim was only imitating - for the sake of appearances - what his father had done that day for his mother. Again, it was all about Tim.

One has to feel loved and cherished in order for romance to take place; a person has to feel good about their marriage. Tim felt sex was romance, but for me, I needed to feel the love and affection that was supposed to exist between a husband and wife. But in our relationship, that was extinct. How could there be romance when one person treated the other person like the dirt under their shoes? How could the romance of lovemaking survive if a person felt tension all the time and knew that the one who was supposed to love you would degrade and harm you? How could a person feel romantic and secure when there were no endearments heard but only put downs? How could romance endure without understanding, sensitivity and happiness? How could love and romance continue to grow when there was nothing to nourish and feed it? With coldness, fear and despair consuming me 24/7, how could romance ever have a chance to flourish and bloom? How could a marriage survive with nothing solid to stand on and nothing to sustain it?

17. Day Care and Work

When my son started kindergarten I decided I needed to be home for the children. We went through a number of daycare facilities, which didn't work out. The ones that did the people moved away. I thought it would be easier to stay home. The children loved the idea of mommy being home for them when they got home from school. They even had their share of being sick in order to stay home with me. I had a big state inspection and was given my state license to take care of children in my house. I was a licensed day care provider, (Little Tykes Day Care). You are probable thinking, I was nuts bringing in more children with that monster in the house. But it worked out well because most of the children had already gone home by the time Tim returned home from work. If he was home he spent his time in the garage and had no interaction with the day care children. The day care worked out well for quite a while. Every Monday I would bring up the high chair and play pens and put the toys out for the children and on Fridays would store it all away again. I ran my business for ten years and loved working with the children. But after ten years of Barney and Sesame Street I needed adult conversation. I was getting burnt out. By this time my children were tired of sharing their house and mom with other children. They wanted their house and mom back and I didn't blame them. The children were a positive diversion for me and I was able to love, teach and nurture them. Slowly I was becoming a person again.

Tim was on me all the time. He hated the toys around and complained that we never had a day without day care and that I was picking up toys and clothes even on weekends. He would complain that the house was not clean and in order, or that the laundry wasn't done. He didn't understand that I had children to watch and six little ones was a hand full. Planning snacks, lunches and activities took up time as well as cleaning up spills and picking up after the children. And there was an endless amount of diapers that had to be changed. He was unable to see any positives. During the day I would do a few things when the children were napping. The dishes had to be done and I would fold towels once in a while. Little ones spilled lots of juice and milk. But most times I worked on projects to do with the children. Art was a favorite of the children and mine, so I made lots of pictures for them to color. We played outside in the nice weather and went for walks once in a while. I even had a little pool the children could play in. I would play ball with them; and took lots of pictures that the mother's loved. Tim didn't see the use of all this and didn't want me to continue wasting my time.

I finally applied at a temp service to shut him up and went to work. A few months later I was hired full-time. I went to work on third shift a very hard shift to work. Trying to sleep during the day and stay up at night was new to me. Everything was backwards. I would get home about 7:30 am and go to bed after making sure the children were off to school. They were older now, junior high and high school, but still sometimes needed a push. On occasion they missed the bus, so I'd give them a ride to school. I had to be up by 4:30 and make sure supper was ready just the same; chores and laundry had to be done and still I had to find time to spend with Tim. My children really suffered. Again I began to get more and more depressed and didn't want anything to do with my family. By my second year at work things were desperate and unbearable. Things had to be his way and only his way. My son was in trouble all the time and Marti was keeping to herself. I would go for walks and not know how I got there or back again. I would be wide-awake one minute and sound asleep the next because of the antidepressants the doctor put me on. But that didn't stop Tim from wanting sex. Now his complaint was that we were weekend lovers. Our schedules didn't match anymore and with him demanding me to be up when he got home it didn't give me much time in the evenings to do the necessary things around the house. And the last thing I wanted to do before work was to be degraded by having repulsive sex with him. I always made sure the lights were out and would usually cry. I hated him touching me now with a passion. My skin felt like it was crawling with every disgusting, degrading touch of his. Nothing good, just creepy feelings, after I would curl up in my tiny little spot and cry my silent tears. Sometimes if he got home early he would come in the bedroom wake me up and climb on top of me. I would just lie there so it would be done and over with. I certainly despised him and hated everything about him.

I started making friends at work and wanted to do things with them. *No way. Not allowed.* We don't associate with people from work, "work and home don't mix", is what I was told. But he could bring his friends home. This was another way of trying to keep me isolated. I was at home all those years with no friends, only his friends and doing what he required, when he wanted. I would defy him and go out once in a great while, but I would get reprimanded and pay the usual high price for my insolence. To me it was worth it because for a short time I would be free from a life of disaster and turmoil that kept me captive. One time I decided to have a few friends over for breakfast after work. What harm could it do? I would be at home where he could keep his ever-vigilant eyes on me and he could meet the people I was associating with at work. We all worked on the same production line and agreed it would be nice to get together. My house was the closest and most centrally located to everyone so we decided to meet there. Everyone brought something different to eat and we had a pot of coffee and juice too. When Tim got up my friends were there, we invited him to join us, but he refused and sulked out to do errands. My friends! It felt great to say I had friends. They stayed about an hour then headed home for bed after a long night. Maurice decided to stay a while and chitchat. He and I sat at the table talking, time just going by. Tim came home a few hours later and was highly irritated. What did I do this time? I could tell by his attitude that I was in trouble once more. I was in the battle zone once again for Hyde was in his eyes piercing through me. I knew without a doubt, and I felt it deep within my soul. Maurice stayed a few more minutes then left as we were both extremely tired. When he left Tim let me have it. Yelling at me, threatening me and berating me. How dare you sit here with another guy, a stranger, here alone in *my* house? I don't like it, or him, and you ***will never*** do that again. I told him we were just friends and what harm was it to sit at the kitchen table with the doors wide open in broad daylight talking. He didn't want to hear it and so that was the first and last time I ever had people over. Because he now only had a 99% control over me since I started working, he tried even harder to keep me more isolated and alone.

I was changing and he didn't like it. He would accuse me of having an affair, or say there was someone else. Yes, there was *something* else, a life outside of 1 Mitchell Drive. He was fighting to keep control, to keep me cut off and under his thumb but it was slowly slipping away and he didn't like it in the least little bit. He had to be in command so the iron fist was hitting us each day with more destructive, calculating force than ever. The more threatened he felt, the higher the price we all paid. Tim's temper was persistent, the disparaging remarks continuous and his fist slammed into Victor more frequently, because of his insecurities.

18. *Explosive Situation*

It was the holiday season and things were extremely difficult in our house. The level of ever-looming tension in the house was fierce and disheartening. My hands shook continually and my anxiety level was skyrocketing out of control. Weight was falling off me a pound a day; I was constantly feeling sick, could not sleep and cried all the time. Marti and Victor now in high school no longer smiled; they jumped at any little thing, were violent towards each other incessantly and gave the impression of hating anyone and anything. We had Thanksgiving with Tim's family as always. We started out sharing holidays with both sides of our families, but as the years went on the separation began and all the holidays were spent with his side. I didn't see it until it was too late; so calculating bit by bit he slowly isolated the children and me from my family. So scared and paralyzed for so many years I didn't see it happening. It was Saturday night after Thanksgiving and we decided to put up the Christmas decorations. I thought it might brighten our gloomy atmosphere and give us just a little bit of happiness for a brief time. But it was not to be. I could hear Tim berating and yelling at Victor about something to do with tools. I was in the living room putting lights on the tree when Marti came in with a horrified expression on her face and said to me, "*Mom dad just hit Victor with the hammer.*" **What!!**

Without a moment's hesitation I immediately went into the kitchen where I could see Victor and his father at the end of the hall. Tim had the hammer raised up toward Victor and was yelling at him about it being damaged. He was so angry it was ingrained in his body language. With a few inches separating the two of them Tim with a menacing stance so rigid and straight was demoralizing Victor. Victor just stood there being bullied once again only this time his hands were clenched tight at his side. Crystal clear on his once again pale face was fear and hatred. For months Victor had been working on his eagle project required by the scout board in order to make Eagle Scout. The troop helping Victor with this project was in the process of restoring and transforming an old firehouse into what is now The Blue Heart Museum. Participants of the project had brought different types of tools to the work site for all to use as well as Victor who brought in a stool and a hammer. Tim kept demanding that Victor tell him how the hammer got broken, Victor didn't know. He told his father many people were using all the tools left around and that anyone could have picked it up used it and damaged it. I was shocked by what I saw next. Tim again demanded an answer from Victor about the hammer and then struck him in the chest with it. Just a tap not hard but I couldn't believe it. What was going to happen next? I stood there shocked. Did I just see him strike my son with the hammer? Astonishingly, with me standing there, he struck Victor a second time. I don't know how it happened, but I was in between the two of them in a flash. I don't remember moving or even taking a step. Yet there I was between them, Tim glaring down at me hammer still held tightly in his hand. All I could think of was Tim smashing Victor with the hammer hard and killing him. I knew his temper and was desperately afraid something worse would happen. He would be out of control in a moment's time. I knew about his behavioral patterns and his temper all too well. I remember looking him square in the eyes yelling at him demanding that he leave my son alone. I grabbed the hammer and would not let it go. Tim was furious. I could see the rage in his eyes and the hatred on his now red face. He snarled at me telling me to let go and leave, but I refused. I told him not while you have the hammer I'm not. With fearlessness I never knew I had and persistence I yelled *put it down!!* With a growl in his voice, he demanded, "Samantha get out of the way now." I was not letting go of a dangerous weapon in the hands of this violent monster. I screamed at him, *NOOO!!* I was shaking the whole time and sweat was running down my back. Fear and dread growing increasingly with each breath I took. It was hard to breathe. My chest was tight, constricting, my anxiety level through the roof. I knew with absolute certainty it was only a matter of a moment that something terrible would happen. It was going to be dreadful, we were not safe. Tim is five feet eight inches tall and my son is six feet tall. I am just four feet eleven inches tall, and I was in-between the two of them. Still I didn't yield to his piercing eyes and his continuing threats that were trying to intimidate me. It was a stalemate neither of us would move. I stayed my ground and would not retreat no matter what the consequences. I could see him getting angrier and angrier every second but still I held my ground. Finally hoping to quell the situation, I pushed the hammer away demanding and strongly advising him to put it down. Tim was so angry it was consuming him and nothing was going to stop the rage that was approaching and coming like a tornado. I didn't care, I was resolute, he wasn't getting to my son again, and I had-had enough.

Marti had been watching the terrifying episode from the kitchen. She must have followed me after telling me about the initial hit with the hammer. I didn't know she was there until she started screaming at her father. Marti shrieked at her father, *"why don't you pick on me for a change, you always pick on him why don't you just stop? Hit me! Come on, hit me! Why don't you hit me?"* She thought, because she was his little girl, that he would stop. She thought she could divert the attention away from her brother and never dreamed he would throw the hammer at her. Tim yelled something at her about shutting up and taunted her by asking, "you want me to pick on you?" "Okay then," he said, and Tim proceeded to *hurl the hammer at our daughter*, making a direct hit when it crashed down on her foot. It was so vengeful and quick that I never saw him raise his arm to throw it at her. She started screaming and crying and doubled over in sheer pain. She couldn't put her foot down because of the agonizing pain. At this time we all became hysterical, crying, yelling and screaming at each other. Tim was still yelling at me to move he was determined to get his hands on Victor. I still stood firm with no understanding of where my courage was coming from. He kept telling Victor that this was his entire fault. Tim warned me again, Samantha get the hell out of the way. ***I'll move you if I have to!*** The next thing I knew, Tim grabbed me by the neck and threw me across the room. So swift was his action that I didn't see his hand come up to my neck. When I opened my eyes, I was on top of my son in my daughter's room with Tim coming at us. (He had thrown me about ten feet across the room). He came into the room with clinched fist and focused his menacing eyes on us. I had to keep him away from us. All I could think to do was just start kicking and screaming. I was beyond frightened. He was totally out of control and looked like he was actually going to kill one of us. On this night, nothing was going to deter me from keeping my children safe. I kept screaming at him to get out that I hated him. I got up and we continued hollering at each other while he was still trying to get to Victor, but I was vigilant; his guard and stayed between them. I knew I couldn't hold Tim off much longer, so I told Victor to get out, go over to his grandparents and tell them that we desperately needed help. Victor knew from the look on my face and the fear in my voice that he had better go for his sake as well and for ours. As he ran out the door his father yelled, "If you leave, you leave with only what you have on your back". I went into the kitchen, Tim into the bedroom and Marti went into the living room. Five minutes later his parents showed up, fear written all over their faces. They wanted to know what the hell was going on. I was shaking violently and sobbing; Marti was crying and limping as she could put no pressure on her foot because of the severe pain she was in.

Tim's parents said Victor came over shaking, and all upset because of the fight going on. None of us could speak. We were dreadfully shaken by the inexcusable situation that had just taken place. Tim told them that nothing was going on and that they should mind their own damn business; but they knew differently. There was something going on, and they knew it. They said their grandson doesn't show up after dark in a panic-stricken condition for nothing. After a few minutes of calming down I told them some of what went on and told them that I didn't want Tim here in the house any more. His father looked at me with anger written on his face pointed a finger and said, "***You are the only one that can make that happen.**"* They didn't get much more out of us, I was afraid of what Tim would do next, he was still fuming and now someone else was involved and interfering. When they left they said they would send Victor home later after he was calmed down. Tim was really pissed that I sent Victor over there, I knew what he would do, and he was so out of control my son would without doubt have ended up in the hospital or dead. The decorations were forgotten; we were to shaken up and distraught to continue with such a small effort for happiness. Happy holidays to us one more year. Why didn't I call 911? Could he have really kept the children from me? Were the black clouds lifting even though I felt so bad? My daughter said she was going bowling with friends. I knew she couldn't bowl but I let her go, she needed to get out of the house; away from the darkness and dread. She needed to be some place safe, some place she could breathe and let loose her bottled up emotions. Certain friends knew what was going on in our lives and she would be able to confide in them.

I found out a few days later that her father broke two of her toes with the hammer. Her toes were so black and blue and swollen she could hardly walk. When he found out he said he didn't mean to do it but, he should not have thrown the hammer in the first place. No, he should not have been threatening my son with it in the first place. We went to bed that night not talking to each other. I told him I needed time to think, to digest what had just transpired, that this was an explosive situation and everything was escalating out of control and something needed to be done. This time when I curled up in my little corner of the bed I still cried, but now I knew I would not go on any longer and I knew that my children would not and could not suffer any more by the hand of this brutal monster, their father.

I went to work Sunday night; I was doing okay and then all of a sudden I got extremely hot, sweat started running down my back, I started shaking and feeling nauseous. I felt like I was going to faint so I went into the ladies room splashed cold water on my face gripped the sink to steady myself and started crying. Maurice saw me take off and sent Mary to check on me. She was my best friend at work and helped me through very dark and miserable times. She calmed me down, and I went back onto the production floor where I told Maurice what had happened. He and another friend were clearly shocked and upset about the ordeal. There was a scratch on my neck I hadn't realized was there and they knew Tim hit me. They knew I was in danger and that I was extremely jumpy and afraid all the time. I was miserable all night; I didn't know what to do or where to turn. My head was swimming with anxieties and my body was racked with pain. Weakness and despair was enveloping me. I felt like I could not breathe; I was suffocating, constantly on guard looking over my shoulder, with no hope left in me. I was reduced to feeling like a little mouse, I was so scared and easily intimidated.

When we left work, Maurice took me to his house and called the Network Against Domestic Abuse (NADA). All the years of abuse and turmoil and I never knew the Network was just two miles from my house. I was in no condition for anything so he made an appointment for me. I went in that week and talked to a counselor. She told me I was not alone; of group sessions I could attend and about having code words and a safe plan in case something else happened. She suggested that I might need psychiatric help and most important was that I needed to keep the children safe. It was a long quiet week neither Tim nor I speaking to the other. On guard vigilantly not knowing what was to come next. Just the cold quiet stares coming from his stone eyes as he passed by. Something was different and he sensed it. After a week of silence he came home from work and after supper he sent the children to their rooms. He said he wanted to talk. I didn't want to. It was his 40th birthday and I had a party for him planned, but had canceled it because of the severity of our ongoing situation. He insisted we talk. I sat at the kitchen table shaking violently; breathing hard and feeling faint. He was trying to intimidate me but it was not going to work this time. His reign of terror, cruelty and abuse was over with once and for all. No apology, nothing pertaining to the disastrous night, which he inflicted upon us, was mentioned. He started by saying "you wanted time so here it is now talk."

I can't remember most of what was said. But he asked me if I wanted him there anymore. I cried, even though I hated him now, feared him and had no respect for him any longer it still hurt to say what I knew I had to. It was the hardest thing I had to do but I gathered up my strength and said *"Tim my love for you no longer exists and I don't want you here anymore. The children and I are terrified of you all the time and don't want to live in this hellhole of an existence any longer."* It was my dreams of a good relationship that I was crying over, the love that never existed, the father that never was and the broken dreams that would never come. I know that now. He looked crushed and maybe even shocked. Then looked at me with tears in his eyes, he went into the bedroom packed a bag and left without another word. He went over to his folk's house where he stayed until after the divorce.

Tim would call every morning to say, "I love you," and hang up. Victor and I talked about this incident years later. I asked him what he felt and what he thought had happened. I was shocked by what he had to say. He said that when I had been standing between him and his father that his own anger was growing. He said that when his father took hold of my neck, that he just snapped. All he could see was the terrible years of constant abuse to him, Marti and me. He said that it was not going to go on any longer. When his father had his hands around my neck, Victor balled his own hand into a fist and pulled back in order to strike - Victor was going to pound the shit out of his father once and for all. He said that at that moment his father could see the rage in Victor, which was precisely when Tim threw me across the room, making sure he took out Victor to prevent him from taking a swing. Victor said it was a good thing that I landed on him because of the force with which his father threw me. He said that, without a doubt, I would have broken something because I was at least two feet off the ground. He also said that if it had not been for me landing on him that he certainly would have beaten his father to within an inch of his life. Through the years, I always said that I hoped Victor would pound his father. Every time I said it, Tim would threaten me and say it would never happen. It is sad to say, but I don't think I would have stopped my son if he had the chance to pound his father. He told me that while he was with his grandparents that his father had told him, "If you leave, you leave with only what you have on your back, and don't come back." I know now why Victor was struggling so desperately when I landed on him. All the years of abuse had finally bubbled up and boiled over. Now it was his turn to let loose. He was consumed with hate, furious with his father and wanted to hurt him. In this same conversation he told me of a few more incidents that happened while I was out of the house when he was younger.

I was bowling one Monday night with his grandmother. His father made hamburgers. He put onions in them and many spices that Victor did not like. Victor liked plain food. He was not eating so his father kept yelling at him. "Why aren't you eating?" Victor told him that he didn't like the stuff in the burgers. His father said, "Oh, you want more ketchup. There's no ketchup on it." Tim got the ketchup out and forced Victor's head back and squeezed the bottle pouring the ketchup down his throat, choking and gagging him. His father then shoved him and told him to take a shower and go to bed. Victor said he had ketchup all over his face and down the front of his clothes. Another occurrence was when his father made corn beef and cabbage. Victor being a picky eater didn't like the cabbage and wasn't eating it. Victor had a loose tooth. His father got mad at him for not eating and belted him in the mouth. The tooth was no longer loose. His father knocked it out. Victor went to the bathroom to rinse his mouth of blood and was again sent to bed without supper.

19. The Separation

I found a journal I'd been keeping after we separated. I needed somehow to keep track of my thoughts in order to keep myself straight and to keep from going out of my mind. The entries are copied as were written by a very depressed woman. There are many confusing, fractured thoughts and unfinished sentences contained in these pages.

Dec 25, 1997

Christmas morning. He showed up at 9:30 with a sour puss on his face a mile long. Opened gifts, then asked if he could give me a kiss and hug. When I said no. He left. Stayed ½ hour.

Christmas was rough; the in-laws came over Christmas Eve and gave me my gifts it was hard for all of us. I stayed home Christmas day while the children went over their grandparents in the morning. It was my choice. I felt I didn't belong there anymore. To my surprise all the brothers and sisters in laws and nieces and nephews showed up later that day. They still had hope that things would work out. But how could they. I don't think they realized all he put us through, not only that night, but for years and years.

The phone rang later that afternoon. The children and I were spending time together before we went over to my folks for Christmas dinner. It was Tim. He wanted the photo albums of the children. I told him I would look for them. I was in a panic. Even though he wasn't living with us anymore, he still had control and I still feared him. It was an automatic panic that came over me. I was looking all over the place for the albums he wanted, I was shaking and sweating and as usual was struck with panic if I didn't do this right. To my surprise, my daughter stopped me in my tracks. She said," look at yourself mom, you are still doing it. You are jumping just because he called and asked for something. Stop, you don't have to do this anymore." While she said this to me she had my face cradled in her hands. It was – I can't even explain the feeling. First to hear that I didn't have to jump anymore, but more so, to know how much my daughter recognized this in me and took control of the situation. I guess it was freeing, to know that I didn't have to jump but was still scared because of the past.

Dec 27, 1997

Came over to do bills, will not pay car payment, cable or phone, will only pay ½ of other bill. After doing the bills he mentioned the music box he gave me for Christmas. I told him that I said not to spend a lot of money. He got up and slammed the checkbook on the table and said he was trying to get a point across. That he lived on three dollars for two weeks because of that music box. It's funny because I knew he was just trying to get me back he never bought me a music box before only if someone badgered him about it. He always said I had enough and didn't need one from him. I have a large collection of music boxes from all different countries. Hawaii, Germany, Australia, China, California, New York, Vermont and are just a few of the places in which the music boxes are from.

Dec 30 1997

He had Marti put a letter on my pillow for me to read. Called to ask if I read it and got mad cause I didn't want to talk about it.

After the holidays I went in to talk to my boss. I was having a hard time walking since I was thrown across the room. The doctor said I had bursitis, which was activated in the fall. Some days I couldn't stand at all which meant I couldn't do my job. I didn't want the boss to think I was just goofing off, so I went in and explained what was going on. She was in tears herself and gave me the number to a help line. It was through the help line that I was able to obtain a lawyer.

Jan 3 1998

Tim wanted the children to go over and watch movies. They went over and when Marti said she had to leave at 7 o'clock (four hours later) Tim got mad. Told them both to leave and said if they want him out of their lives just to say so. Both children came home very upset and crying.

Jan 4, 1998

He called seven or eight times before I got up. Tim came over to get car to wash it. We got into an argument. He brought up the letter again, told me it was so out of character to leave five children unattended on New Year's Eve. Call children 18 and older. His mother called New Year's morning asking for me. I wasn't home. So Tim called about five minutes later asking for me. Won't believe Marti. Was upset because I wasn't home? He brought that up again. Proceeded to yell at me about the letter and his feelings. Doesn't understand why I feel as I do. All about how he feels left out, wants his family back, keeps bringing up Anger Management, saying he has to see how much it is going to cost. When we did the bills last time he said he was only going to pay certain ones. Asked why I told my brother that he was leaving me high and dry. Never said that. Told my brother what he said about the bills. Now he says he never said that. Blaming me for the children not wanting to spend time with him. Says I am making them feel guilty. I tell them all the time if they want to see him they can. Just not at the house. He was mad because they were late. Blamed me. I told them to get going. Sure enough he got mad. Says he is going to change and control his temper but he stood there yelling at me and blaming me for everything. Says Victor's temper isn't his fault. Can't see where Victor gets his temper. I felt very nervous with him there. Lost two pounds again in a day because he upsets me so much. Hands are shaking badly. Asked me if I married him because I was pregnant or not and to think about it. Trying to lay guilt trip on me. Saying how everything is my fault. Says I hurt him all the time because I don't want to talk to him.

Went for test after he threw me across the room. Have bursitis in my hip. It was inactive until now. Will act up whenever my back does. Also have liver trouble because of lose of weight. May be because of gall bladder. Going for ultrasound Friday the 9th at 9:15. Doesn't think group counseling is any good. He talked to some people that told him it is a waste of time. I start Monday night the 5th of Jan.

Wednesday we go for family counseling. The children need it badly. They don't want to go after Saturday. They were told they have to go even if it is just once. He told them, that he feels they should call every day or night to ask how he is and how his day went and so he can talk to them. Came over wanted keys to Concorde to wash it. He said what's the matter you don't want me to wash it? The way he said it I felt very threatened. So I gave him the keys. I felt very nervous with him in the house. Says it is his house, then corrects himself and says our house. ALL ABOUT CONTROL!!!!!!!!!!

Evening Jan 5 1998

Told me to have Marti call him. Wanted to talk things over. Said he was going to take her out to dinner. She left at 5:10. Then she called a short time later to have Victor go over. He rented movies for them to watch. Don't know what happened have to talk to children.

Jan 7 1998

Family session Victor thinks I'm not giving Tim a fair chance. Feels it's his entire fault. Tim says I use lack of judgment on leaving Marti and friends home New Years Eve. AGAIN BROUGHT UP THE PARTY. Counselor says have to show trust and that she is 18 years old. Everyone does not want to go back. Tim said." what I don't have a say in this?" They left and I told the counselor about my medical problems and that as soon as it is straightened out that I will be filing for a divorce. He said good luck and that his main concern is for the children. Told Tim to listen to me. Told Tim I want him to leave me alone. Counselor said if it is what I want and need then he should. I could compromise and write him a note if I have to contact him about the children or house. I feel very up tight. Counselor told children that I was very strong for doing this and that they should support me. MAD Every time he tells me something, I feel like he's trying to make me feel guilty. Like tonight he said that he is totally out of scouts. Like it is supposed to matter. Like I'm supposed to feel sorry now because he has nothing. Too bad, that was his choice.

Jan 8, 1998

Victor and Marti had a big fight. Went to group session. It was very good though it made me nervous. Said I should watch when driving to see if he is following me, have phone in my room. A bag packed and when I serve papers. DON'T BE HOME. The children are not talking to each other. Marti got speeding ticket 87 MPH $170.00 Things are just getting worse.
Jan 11, 1998

He wanted the children to go over. Because I forgot to have Victor call yesterday, Tim got really mad. Hung up on Victor. I called him to see what was going on because the children got upset. Told me not to call if I had anything to say write it in a note. My words not his. Got mad when I sent some of his things over. Said to stay out of his stuff. Proceeded to get mad at the children when he emptied the bag out. Sent me a letter. Said he can't handle the emotional up and down of talking to me and to just write. Send the bills over he will write them out and send them back. Children come back upset each time they see him. Marti pointed out how he doesn't seem to want to change. He talks big but his actions show otherwise.

Jan 12 1998

He had Marti go with him to a wake for Bruno's wife. Marti never even met the lady she also had to drive. He asked what I was doing with all my over time money. Worked one week of it. Haven't even got the check yet. He told her he thinks I am saving it for a lawyer. He shouldn't keep at her. She always comes home upset. Both group sessions I have been to suggest a safety plan. Especially when papers are served. Leader said to make sure I know when they are served because he is going to blow. I should not be around. Cleaned all his things out of my bedroom. Also his cars out of cabinet and put my music boxes in them. Victor saw it and said when dad sees it he will get mad. I wish they could hear their own words. He keeps calling my sister and asking questions about me. Like what am I thinking, what is going through my head? Called my brother a few times too asking the same. He never even bothered with my family before. Have to work on priorities for in 2-week session. Doctors tomorrow find out about the ultrasound. Marti will be back at school on Monday and Victor has agreed to counseling. Have to get a lot of positive reinforcement for the children. Especially Victor. Lots of men for a good influence. Counselor said it is good that I am making Marti pay for the ticket and that I took the car away. *Do not* tell Victor he is like his father or has his father's temper. It will bring him down. He will only see how bad his father is and internally think he is just as bad. Tell him he does have a temper, but it is his temper and he needs to learn to control it. Keep telling him good things, reinforcement.

Needs lots of good male influence. Marti needs to make sure she talks to the sister at the college. She needs to stay focused. When this all first happened, Victor and I got along great. He did things without being asked and wanted to help me. The day Marti got home. Forget it. He has refused to do a thing and gives me nothing but trouble. Ask the counselor about it. She said when Marti came home, it took away Victor's ability to take care of me and have charge for a change. The younger child usually feels threatened. Once she leaves he will probably go back to being nice.

Jan 14, 98

Marti told me her father is going to a party Friday night with a female companion. He told her absolutely not to tell me.

Jan 15, 98

He wrote me another note. Truly doesn't understand.

Jan 26, 98

Well last week on the 23rd I was rushed to emergency. Was in excruciating pain for over two hours. Was having a gall bladder attack. On the 24th it was taken out and all I did was get grief from everyone. He was pissed off because I didn't want him at the hospital. Told my sister if I wanted him to hate me I was doing a good job of it by not letting him see me. Mrs. D was mad because Jody (my boss) called her and she didn't know a thing and was embarrassed about it. Everyone thinks of themselves. I was the one having an operation.

No date

Saw him yesterday coming out of the credit union on North Drive. He is up to something.

Well he will get a surprise in a week or so because next Thursday I see the lawyer. I will start the paper work for my divorce. It is scary, but I feel it has to be done. I don't want to live in fear any more and I don't love him anymore. I can say I have not for a very long time. Just been going through the motions.

Jan 27, 98

Got another letter. He stopped his guard check from going into savings account. Also changed credit union, Allotment now going into another credit union. Only in his name. Said I can have any money just ask. Won't keep any from me, but I have to ask him for it. Refuses to pay cable bill.

Jan 29, 98 Went and started divorce proceedings. Tim will be served

Monday or Tuesday. Have it planned to go over Dan's with Victor for the night.

Jan 30, 98

He is home today. Phone rang, I picked up and no one there. Has happened before. Makes me very nervous. Don't' know if it is him or not. Yesterday the lawyer tore up the power of attorney he had on me. Will be changing title to vehicle. Will be taking back my maiden name.

Jan 31, 98

Was talking to Marti the other day. She told me that he lectured her all the way back to college. Not yelling just saying how she is supposed to set a good example for her brother. Telling her she was reckless and being a drunk. She was very unhappy about it. She is coming home next weekend and doesn't want her father to know. She doesn't want to see or talk to him. Victor on the other hand is getting along great with him. Spent the night over there last night. They work on models and watch movies. His boom box is missing. He either gave it to his father to use or he broke it in one of his temper tantrums and is hiding it. He came home in a good mood. Usually he is aggravated when he comes home. He did mention he had to leave by 2 o'clock because his father is going out tonight. When I left to go to Mini Mart he was in front of me in his truck. Was all decked out, had his good coat on and his hair was done up. Tried to get it out of Victor but he told him not to say a word. Not the first time he said not to say a word. Told Marti the same thing a few weeks ago. He was going to a party and taking a female companion with him. Says he starts his group session this week. He wants me back and wants me to love him again. It is not going to work. I do not love him and have nothing else to give him.

How do I feel about the divorce? I am scared. Don't know what to expect, I am relieved that it is finally in the works. Through all kinds of soul searching, many hours of driving, loud music, staring at pictures and going through things over and over again in my head. I know I do not love him anymore. I do not respect him and have nothing left to give him. I don't think I hate him, but I do fear him and still have a lot of anger towards him. I don't think I can get past what he has done to the children and me. He has taken everything from me. Self-respect, self-esteems, has controlled everything for the last 18 1/2 years. NO MORE I feel stronger. Scared at times. But I don't feel like that scared little mouse anymore. As hard as it may be some days, I will get through it. And through it all the upset with the children the battles with Victor, Marti going back to school.

I AM HAPPY. As the old saying goes - pictures say a thousand words. I just developed about 15 rolls of film. I have a smile, but it is not a happy one. I have two pictures that were taken since this all started. And those have a real happy smile in them. I could not believe it until someone pointed it out. The gall bladder attack took a lot out of me. I had a lot of pain and surgery. Now I am on my feet again, and going back to work. Made it through with the help of friends, family and myself. I am eating better now. Not great but better. Weight is staying between 104 and 106 pounds. So all in all, I am surviving and I am a survivor with more to handle.

A letter to my brother and his wife:

Hi Everyone,

Well I am back on my feet again. Going back to work February 1 Two weeks home was plenty for me. Don't want to have to go through that again. I want you to hear it from me. Tim will be served divorce papers this week. I have made up my mind. I want to be happy. Cannot be with a man I do not love or respect anymore. So now it begins. Hopefully it will not be a battle. I just want to get it done and over with so I can get on with my life. I hope you understand why I have to do this. My children and myself are my main concern now. Have to do what is best for the three of us now. I know I am doing the right thing. I will not look back. I have done a lot of soul searching over the last few weeks. I now know that I have not been happy for a very long time. I go to two support groups now. Through these groups I have learned a lot about myself. I am a strong person and will continue to get stronger with each day. Sure some days are good and some bad. But that is how I take it. One day and one step at a time.

Love Samantha

Feb 2, 98

He was served with papers. Really mad. Called a number of times.

Feb 5, 98

He talked to his lawyer. He is being really nice. He will keep the house if he can.

Feb 7, 98

Was showing Marti the phone bill. She pointed out something really interesting. The phone will ring and no one is there. So I stared 69. Came up on the phone bill as 745-xxxx. His number. Will have to keep track of it.

Feb 8, 98

He came over to go through the house. Made lists out of what we want. Was nervous with him there. Could feel my hip going on me. I am at work now and it really hurts. He told me that the wagon, trailer and boat are mine, to sell them and that the money will go towards the Concord. He is making a stink about the black truck.

Feb 9, 98

He has to get a new lawyer, Conflict of interest because they did the wills. He will see the new lawyer today. Already said that nothing we agreed on is any good. Told me if I go after his retirement plan then everything changes. I believe he will get real nasty if I do. Also said something to the effect of me not being able to stay in the house after the divorce so I can find a place.

Feb 10, 98

Talked to Tim today. He saw his new lawyer and he laid it on the line. He has to split everything down the middle including his pension and 401k. , Which is $30,000? He is not happy. Was told he will have to pay child support and alimony for 91/2 years. We will be selling the house. ***Told me to put it on market right away.*** Will ask lawyer about that. Said he will only talk to me thru the lawyers. Also said this is my entire fault. I want the divorce. He wants to get back together. He wants to work things out. TOO BAD!

Feb 28, 98

Victor was very upset, spent time with his father again. Says that he has changed and I am not being fair. Telling me all I feed him is noodles. Not true, he eats everything. We straightened things out.

Mar 1, 98

Talked to Tim, says he will contest the divorce if he has to pay alimony. Wants the black truck and money out of this. Telling me I have to change my name.

Mar 2, 98

Got e-mail from Marti. Tim told her I said she is melodramatic. She is so mad. Says I am high and mighty and that I have been lying to her and that I am leaving him nothing. Boy he really is working on them. Well we will see what the lawyer has to say.

Mar 4 98

Freaking jerk told Marti I said she is melodramatic. She has been giving me such an attitude. This SUCKS so badly. All I can do is think about all this shit. All I want to-do is cry and I HATE IT. Will be picking her up Friday and hopefully we can talk.

Mar 6, 98

He called. Telling me that he is getting a different job and it will be less money. Says that I may even have to pay him alimony. I DON'T THINK SO. I have the house and Victor. Keeps asking about getting back together. When I said I didn't trust him he went off on me. Said I cheated on him, that I'd have someone in here in a year's time. I am a liar and he doesn't trust me.

Mar 7, 98

Came over to do taxes. He said he was sorry for going off and that it certainly didn't show me that he is trying to change. This is true. He can't understand why. Told him I don't trust him and that we have no respect for each other. He keeps saying how we are like his parents and I agree. I told him that all I can see is more of the same 20 years from now and I DON'T want it. I don't' trust him and I don't want to live in fear. He says I didn't give counseling a fair chance. Oh well. There is nothing for me to save with him.

I DO NOT LOVE HIM AND CANNOT GIVE ANYTHING ELSE BACK. DON'T HAVE ANYTHING LEFT FOR HIM. I am finally getting a backbone and some self-respect and I won't lose it again by going back to him. All he can see right now is the money and possessions. That's all he talks about. Having things. You can have everything, but without

LOVE forget it. I was so uptight last night that my cough was back. Had people over and coughed most of the night. Our anniversary was in April, it was 19 years together. He sent me a card and roses. Like the music box he gave me for Christmas, Tim never got me flowers. I threw them away, my son took them out of the trash and put them in a vase and said, "at least he is trying". Then when I talked to him he told me that he had plans to take me on a cruise for our 20th anniversary. I was dumb founded. A cruise of all things, he never listened to me or heard me, because if he did he would have known that I was no way getting on a cruise ship. I am deathly afraid of being surrounded by all that water.

May 5, 98

Well we are supposed to have a court date for June 5th. It is supposed to be with the lawyers. I called my lawyer and he didn't even know anything about it. Just great. Said he will get back to me. It is only 4 weeks away until the date and nothing has even been discussed. Not good. Feeling very nervous and uptight. Feel sick to my stomach, I am at work and I just want to go home. Crawl into bed and not come out. Tim has not even paid me this past Friday. If I ask him he will get mad but I need the money. Victor needs black jeans and white shirts. He got a job, which requires him to wear these things. Plus I have to pay more bills. Paid $2000.00 worth Saturday and still have more. This sucks. He complains that he has to give me $250.00 every two weeks. Big deal. He lives with his folks and has no bills. I have them all. Got the mortgage, car, insurance, utilities and all. He has doctors and credit cards. So what, I am managing but still. Even now it is not fair. Try and try to get ahead and can't do it. Just getting very uptight. Every little thing bothers Victor. And Marti doesn't even come home anymore. She spends the weekends with this 28-year-old guy Tim. They get mad at me because I go out now. All they want is me to stay home in four walls. I won't do it. Soon enough they will be gone and I do not want to be alone. I want a life. And it will start as soon as this divorce is over. Hopefully only months after. Still trying to control me. With money, mind games playing Disney dad. He only thinks of material things.

Emotions, feelings, gentleness, kindness, caring, friendship. He has no idea what these things are and what they mean. What there could have been if he had only treated the children right and me too? For this I am sorry and sad for he didn't care enough. I have no regrets as to my decision. It is the best thing I could have done. He cannot see it. Only sees that he doesn't have control anymore. That is what he wants. He got mad the other day. Victor told him I made a pantry out of the closet in the kitchen. His clothes were in there. What did I do with them? Hey tough. I packed them in boxes and put them down cellar. The good clothes are hanging in the computer room closet. He didn't like it. Said, "So you are pretty sure you are getting the house". Told him I wasn't sure of anything just making things easier for myself. His attitude changed right away. Got uptight and had to hang up. Oh well. Victor should not be telling him these things. It will only cause trouble. He has got to find a way to let this go and to get past it. Wait until Victor spends a lot of time with Tim. He only wants to see what he hopes for. Not what is? How come the victim is always the victim? The blame gets put on that person all the time. Like on this night, I asked Victor to do the dishes while I was sleeping. And of course, he did not. So after supper I asked him to help me. So he was drying and I said they had to be put away to. He got all mad and said that I never stay off his back and that I better lay off. Don't get it. I never got mad, only made a simple statement. He wants everything his way and doesn't want to do a thing. Should be an interesting summer with both of them home. Hopefully he will put forth a good effort at this job and her too. It will keep them busy and away from each other. Marti is totally different. Her schoolroom is spotless. She comes home and her bedroom is a mess. But then she will get off on a tangent and say the family room is a mess and clean it. She really hates her brother's stuff all over the place. But if I ask her to do something she gives me a hard time. Back and forth. She will come in the door and say she loves me. I will say I love you too and she says. "No mom, I mean I really love you." Yet she goes over Tim's all week and I don't hear a thing from her. Though she will make sure I am the one to pick her up on Friday to come home. Today she will go back to school. Have not heard anything from her since Friday. Don't even know if she will stop by. Sometimes she is so irresponsible. Has no, or little, respect for what I say. Well she will have an awakening about the car and her paycheck. She doesn't get so mad when I go out. At first, yes.

They both said I was 40 going on 20, but I have not done anything in a very long time. They have to realize they will be gone in a few years. I think right now they believe I am still supposed to stay home and just look out for them. That is what they are so used to. Well not anymore.

This was the end of my journal.

Tim played many head games with me during this period of time leading up to the divorce. I didn't know if I was coming or going. He threatened me all the time with lawyer lingo. I was constantly calling my lawyer distraught and hysterical. When he was served his papers he was also given a restraining order, which I knew nothing about. Tim was irate at me for that. I told him I knew nothing about it but he again called me a liar. He kept putting me down in front of the children, telling them how I was not being reasonable and telling lies about me. The children in their state of mind, of course would believe him. I talked to my counselor about this and she said just give it time, He is once again playing the Disney dad and eventually they will see the truth, just don't play his games. She also said he is still trying to have the control that is slipping away and he is still trying to intimidate me.

We went to a family counselor once, all we did was scream at each other, and even the counselor said we couldn't get back together until all the issues were resolved. I knew they wouldn't be, I had enough and I wouldn't go back to living in that hellhole for anything. There was a new door opening for the children and me and we would not turn back now. On the way out I told the counselor we wouldn't be back. The marriage was done and I had no more to give; I gave everything I could and more, and now I was empty. He said he understood and wished me good luck.

At first the children were happy about the divorce. They said I should have thrown their father out a long time ago. We got along pretty well at first, and then as time went on they started to get very angry with me for breaking up the family. The children believed that I had torn their family apart even though when I first asked their father to leave they were glad. They knew the misery, turmoil and destruction and even though that is all they knew it was better than nothing. At least it was a family no matter how atrocious it was.

I mentioned my friend Maurice; he was there for me during a miserable time. Tim as always couldn't own up to his own responsibility in this mess, so now he was blaming Maurice for our divorce. He again said I was cheating on him and told the children that is why we broke up. The children, being vulnerable at this time, fell right into the controlling trap once again and believed what their father was saying. By the time the divorce came my son would not talk to me and my daughter was very angry with me. Only sparingly would she talk to me. I tried explaining the gravity of the situation to them, letting them know there was more to what went on in the house than they knew, but they didn't want to hear it.

I was going to a support group and had to write down four things I wanted to change in the next few months. One of the things I wrote down was "control Victor" it wasn't that I wanted to control him but that I wanted him to have control of himself and have some kind of unity and stability in our house.

I left the notebook on the table and Victor read it. This triggered our non-stop conflict with each other. Because of those two little words our war began in earnest and we didn't get along. He thought I was like his father and in no way would he let me control him. He refused to do anything in the house unless it was for his benefit and he too was now threatening me. Victor was destroying my personal belongings, breaking into my bedroom, taking and hiding different things on me. He felt I was lying to him all the time and didn't trust me, because of his father. Tim had drilled it into Victor's head that I was cheating his father out of his portion of the house. Victor told me that when I sold the house that he now wanted, and was demanding, his own share of the money from the sale of the house. That he had it coming to him for everything he put into the house and everything I put him through.

Here is the crushing letter, sent to me by my precious son that tore open my heart.

Dear Mom,

When it comes time for the four of us to go to court, and they ask me who do you want to live it. Well I am certainly not going to pick you. Dad is going to be the word that comes out of my mouth. I can trust him; I can count on him to be there for me, I find it easier to say I love you to him more than you. He always listens to what I say. He respects me and my things, and I am the same way to him. You still think Dad hasn't changed, because you are to conceited, blind, and selfish to realize it. Every time you say something about him you hurt me even more, because what you say is no longer true.

When I move out, you won't have to worry about food or any of my things on the floor again, and I will be of "no" concern to you anymore.

One more thing, tell Maurice to stay out of my life.   Victor

In response to this letter and other concerns of Victor I wrote this letter to Tim. Even though it ate me up inside to write this letter I felt I had to for my son's sake. Tim had never been supportive before but now he wanted his family back and I was hoping that my concerns would not fall again on deaf ears.

Tim,

Concerning the dog, I think I have been very fair in keeping her for the last 8 months. But I feel because of Victor's lack of responsibility that you will have to take her or find a home for her. He never brushes her out. He has only given her two or three baths in the past year and a half. I ask him to put the chair on the couch so she doesn't sleep on it and he just laughs. She smells and I don't want her on the furniture. He leaves her out overnight sometimes, and she knocks the lid off the bucket of food to feed herself, because he hardly does it. He does absolutely nothing around here to show any responsibility at all.

Also, I have an appointment with a psychologist in two weeks. I will be talking to the psychologist to see about getting Victor treatment. He told me your therapist was checking into it. I feel it has been long enough considering what is going on over here.

On a more personal note, he is constantly breaking into my bedroom and taking my personal things. Such things are panties and bras. I have found them in the ceiling tiles of his room torn to shreds. He has a problem; one of many, which I think, should be addressed.

He will more than likely tell you that I am not cooking for him right now. I am trying to get him to take responsibility for himself. I cook meals for him and he cooks more food later. As of right now there are pots and pans sitting in the sink from Sunday. I cleaned his mess that he made and asked him nicely to wash the two pots and a strainer, they are still sitting there. I buy fruit and yogurt for him. Put good meals together for him and he stills eats the junk. I bought three packages of chicken wings for him last week. He ate them in two days beside what else I made for him.

I would appreciate it if you would back me up concerning him. He needs to be responsible and get off his butt. I also told him if his behavior didn't stop that I would let you know about it and also let a psychologist know about it. I have not gotten any backing from the school. They are too busy to see him. The special-needs children come first. I have called many times and have stopped in to see the school psychologist myself. I am going to get this addressed and get him the help that he needs very badly.

Also, if anything else leaves the house without my permission I will call the police. Victor took the small fridge without permission. I know it is yours but I explained to him that it was given to Marti for school, and that I wanted to wait and see what she was going to do. If anything gets broken or he threatens me, I will call the police. He has a very bad attitude and won't listen to anyone. He says he will not let anyone control him or tell him what to do.

Do not confront Victor with this letter. I do not feel it will do him any good. If you want to mention the dog, okay but the rest should be left to a therapist. I expect that you will support me in this effort to better our son. For this to be done, we have to keep in mind that it is for our son. He needs guidance, support and our love. He feels low enough about himself without more being put onto him. If he knows that you know about this it will only make him feel that he has disappointed you. It will be very hard for him to deal with all that he has hidden inside himself.

Samantha

Even though his father had drilled it into his head and repeatedly said things were his fault Victor still wanted to have his father's approval and love. Now I was the bad guy and Victor had no use for his sister either. Marti came over to visit one Saturday; Victor was in a really foul mood, we were arguing as usual. As always they were not getting along but now he was on his father's side and she on mine. She and I were in the family room talking; he came out and demanded that she get the hell out. I told him she didn't have to and that she was always welcome in our house. Victor stood up and took a step toward her. I stood between them and looked him straight in the eyes and told him he would have to go through me first. I had a flash back because I went through this once before with his father and him. He had been under his father's control for so long now he was trying to be in control and be assertive. He was trying to intimidate me, but it wasn't working. He stood there rage on his face with fist clenched by his side and shaking. I wasn't moving and he wasn't going to touch her or me. Victor stomped off in a huff. He knew I was not going to be intimidated and his menacing stance did nothing to deter me from standing my ground yet again. Marti left shortly thereafter. I tried talking to him, but he would not talk. He was disillusioned and very angry with all of us. In my opinion, Victor will always be on guard because he will not let anyone control him. Not at home or at work, he will always be rebellious against a controlling person and situation.

I was still working third shift, so Victor was home alone most of the time. We were fighting so much now that I would make it a point to be in bed before he got home. I just didn't know what to do. All we did was quarrel. One day while I was exercising he asked me to do him a favor. I refused, I was so angry with him. He shoved me off the exercise bike and when I went to go into the kitchen he slammed the atrium door on my leg and almost broke my leg. As much as I did not want to, I had to call his father to come over and talk to him. Tim kept saying what went on in my house, was no longer a concern of his. But I demanded he come over and talk to his son, because it was his fault that Victor was so angry and being belligerent towards me. Another time because I would not take him to work he locked my exercise flyer in the shed and hid the keys on me so I wouldn't be able to use it.

My daughter Marti was at school and having a very hard time dealing with this whole mess. She cried all the time and my phone bill was over $300.00 with calls to Timothy. I ended up going to school with her one day and she resigned. She could not cope with it any longer, but did not move back home. She moved in with Timothy in spite of my disagreeing with her decision. Marti in no way wanted to be in the house of anger and bad memories. Even with her father gone there was still so much turmoil from all that we had endured and all that was still to come.

We all went through a miserable adjustment period and yes at times I was very selfish. I was free for the first time in 19 years and it felt great. I was going over to a friend's house and just having a good time, bowling, movies, roller-skating whatever I could do that I was forbidden to do before. What people don't realize is that just because a man and a woman are friends don't mean they have to sleep with each other. Maurice and I were good friends, something that I can say Tim and I were not. He was a shoulder to cry on, someone to talk to and a soft place to land. It is very rare that two people can have that kind of a relationship and I was very lucky and privileged to have found such a friend and develop such a wonderful friendship.

20. The Divorce

We went for our divorce in August, when I looked around the courtroom there was my son sitting with his grandparents. Victor hid out in the shed until I left for court. He wanted the judge to hear what he had to say. He wanted the judge to know that he wanted to live with his father. My heart sunk, didn't think I could feel much lower than I already did, but I did. The child that I loved with everything in me and protected and guarded and covered for was now turning against me. There he was sitting with the monster that abused him repeatedly over the years. Constantly putting him down, berating him and criticizing him; yet he was on his side believing what he so desperately wanted to hear and feel. After all Victor went through he still wanted and needed his father's approval. My heart broke into a million pieces that day. All I could do was just sit there quietly in that cold courtroom with my lawyer; tears streaming down my face. His father had been drilling it into Victor's head that I was raking him over the coals. That he was losing everything and I was getting everything. This of course was not true. We had to fill out financial affidavits and all kinds of paper work on what we had throughout the marriage. Everything was split 50/50 each. He was mad because I was getting the house. But what Tim failed to tell his family was that I said he could have the house, that I would take my son, myself and our belongings and get an apartment. Tim was calculating played woe is me and did anything and everything to make me look bad. They bought it. His family never once, not one of them ever came over and asked me what happened or tried to talk to me about anything. They just said blood is thicker than water. After all the years of abuse and his parents saying they would always be there for me and the children they just threw me away like old dish water without a look back or a kind word to me. They just took Tim's side and never asked me a thing. I think it was easier for them than facing the truth about their son, Tim. It is hard to face yourself knowing you raised a child who could do this to his family. So, blaming me allowed them to escape the truth.

When we first separated his letters to me were very sweet and he was always begging me to let him come back. He wanted a second chance and he said he had learned his lesson and was going to be a different person. But as time went on I could see he was not changing. His letters to me became very threatening, cold and hard. He would be demanding and by the time the divorce came he was actually blaming me for everything that happened. The situation was out of his control and he was trying very hard to get back at me. He was in a place he had never been before and was unfamiliar to him. He was in a place he had never expected to be.

I was in counseling when we got the divorce. I was diagnosed with *Post Traumatic Stress Disorder* (PTSD) from years of being abused. Because of it I was put on antidepressants, **again**. All I did was cry and shake; I could not sleep, and had nightmares when I did. I felt like nothing and could barely function. He still had a hold on me; the therapist said it was like a large rope. Through the years we weaved it into a thick rope and now it had to unravel strand by strand and it would take a long time. So on this day, that rope would slowly start to unravel. I told my lawyer that I didn't want the abuse brought up; it was too painful and hurtful, he agreed. But when Tim started mistreating and threatening me my lawyer relayed the information about the abuse to his lawyer. Tim's convenient denial of the abuse made it easy for him not to tell his lawyer about it. My lawyer also told Tim's lawyer if Tim didn't behave that he would let the judge know about all the abuse that took place for so many horrible years. When my lawyer walked away Tim's lawyer was laying into him for not telling him the sordid details of what went on in our house. We were divorced on that day.

My son was to live with me and it was ghastly. We fought all the time and couldn't be in the same room together. We took everything out on each other. We didn't know what to do with all our pent up anger and frustrations so we took it out on each other constantly. The next weekend,

Tim came over to move his things out. He was upset that I asked my brother and Maurice over to be there for me. I was still afraid and was told to have a safety plan in place in case something went wrong and to have people around me who would support me. Another friend Jan was over too, she asked me for a secret word in case things got out of hand. We agreed on something about her daughter coming over. If I mentioned it she was to call the police. I needed that plan. Tim's mom was calling me a liar and his sister was making snide comments to me in front of my children. Tim's sister was cantankerous all day giving me a hard time. I realize everyone was upset; it was a bad time for all. But it was not necessary for these adults to demean me in front of my children or to be yelling at me and accusing me of things they didn't know anything about, especially when a discussion never took place as to the specific occurrences. Tim and I were in the living room talking and I was crying. He wanted to keep talking, but I just couldn't. I was distraught; my anxiety level again was on the rise. I was shaking, yet again, and limping because of my hip. Every time I would get upset or stressed the bursitis in my hip would flare up. The therapist said it was my way of dealing with him and his family. My conscious mind could not deal with the constant bombardment by him and his family, so it took its toll on my body. After more tests I found I also have arthritis in my back right above the hip on my left side. Between the bursitis and the arthritis I would be in severe pain whenever stressed out and often unable to walk.

Tim's sister Meg and I started yelling at each other. She was confrontational all day so I finally told her to get the hell out. I kept telling her to leave, she was so argumentative, yelling at me and putting me down. She and I had always been very close. I watched her son for over two years while she was working. I took out a card I had saved over the years that she had given me and shoved it at her. I told her this is what you meant to me. You were like a sister to me, the little sister that I never had but you don't want to hear anything I have to say. Jan called the police. At the time of their arrival we were all out front hollering and screaming at each other. My son put his trembling hands over his ears and screamed that he couldn't take it anymore. Then he went into the house crying. Marti was crying hysterically, Meg went over to console her. I didn't want her near my child. How dare she touch my child after all this time of no one lifting a hand to help us? I went over and gently moved her hand from my daughter and hugged *my* daughter. Tim's father came over and was yelling now. His sister was being a smart mouth and said something nasty. I don't remember what. I then told the police I just wanted her off my property. The police told her to go, but she kept arguing. The officer told her one more time and she would be arrested. She mouthed off as she left. Someone had told Tim to leave when the police were called. I was glad; for once it was not his fault. Even though I didn't love him anymore and I felt nothing, but hate and animosity for him, I didn't want anything bad to happen to him. The monster he is, he is still my children father. But I guess in the long run the situation was actually his fault. I was simply glad that day was over.

After the divorce we tried to cope with everything that came our way. Marti was finally talking to me. She had come over one day and wanted to talk. I told her what I could but not everything. She still didn't know about the sexual abuse to me by her father. All I said was that she had to confront her father about certain despicable things. She did ask her father about the sexual abuse and he told her what he did. It sickened her. The next time she came over she hugged me tight and asked why I didn't' tell her. How could I? It was so degrading and I was ashamed of myself and embarrassed and why add more to what was previously bad. I had put enough on my little girl over the years she surely didn't need to know about this horrible secret that I kept. After the truth of the sexual abuse was out things were better between us. Not great but better.

As for my son, I finally got him into counseling, though he truly believed he didn't need it. Went through about four counselors before he stuck with one, he also went to anger management with a youth group which did him well. This is a page he brought home:

Some of my needs are:

My family, friends,

I feel good when,

I do something that I am proud of,

I try to run from fear, and hate,

I feel frustrated when

I lose something or something doesn't

go my way,

I am afraid of my

Mother choosing the wrong

relationship again,

MY Hopes are:

To get my own family back,

only better than it was before,

My dreams are

a better life in the future,

I feel angry when someone puts me down,

I am happiest when,

I get along with my family,

especially with my day,

I am best at being myself,

WHO AM I???

I AM

Only one person

In a life with

many different

feelings and

fears that can't

always go the way you expect,

So you do your Best

So much hurt and loneliness, He was so afraid of things he could not control and only wanted to be happy. My son wrote this poem and gave a copy of it to his father and to me.

Stepping out of the Darkness into the Light
By Victor Dudley
Darkness was all around
during the day and
through the night always
THERE scaring you.
15 years of this was like Hell.
Wondering, worrying what will happen next.
Worrying about the force that would
hit me like a rock.
The force was like a burning torch
that always set off a dark glow.
Every time I turned it was there.
Running from it was impossible.
A lower force overcame this
Greater force, this lower force
was love. Now love will always
be the greatest force of all.
As the dark glow of the torch
dwindled out, light crept in as
well as love. THE Torch finally
went out and a bright white
light shown in its place.
I don't have to run anymore
because now love will always be
there.

Between Victor's counselor and mine we finally started talking to each other. We learned that if we were upset to walk away and give it time, which we did over and over again. Victor and I were starting to get along, we were talking and I was rearranging my sleeping schedule, so I could be up with him a few days a week. I would make sure that on his night off on the weekend I stayed home with him, so we could have supper together. Maurice had become a big part of my life and was often there on a weekend. But still my son blamed him and even though the three of us would sit at the table for supper Victor would not say a word to him. Maurice understood and gave him his space. He would say hi when he arrived and bye when he left, but still my son would not acknowledge him. I understood, his family fell apart and now here was a new guy where he felt his father should be. Tim did a real head job on the children especially my son. Why should Victor trust another guy, when he couldn't really trust his own father? Oh, he thought he could, but he couldn't.

After a year of him being home alone, and his father constantly putting me down, Victor decided he wanted and needed to go live with his father. Tim repeatedly told him how much money they could save and how good it would be for the two of them. He said everything a 17 year old wanted to hear all his life even though it was not true. They decided to tell me the day after I got back from a trip and the same day I was told my mom was going in the hospital for a quadruple bypass. I was panic-stricken about my mom and now here was another bomb exploding in my face. To suit the fantasies that my son so desperately wanted to be true, Tim again played the Disney dad. Painting a picture of a miserable mom and the so perfect dad was his game. It crushed me every time someone would say something bad about me. I talked to my counselor about it. She again said give it time and don't give into the games. Your children will eventually see things for the truth that they are and will come around to you. Tim got his way again and my son moved in with him. We had a huge moving day, my daughter had moved out before the divorce and came to get what was left of her belongings, Victor was packing his stuff and I was selling the house. It was too much for me to handle by myself. I didn't want to stay with all the bad memories and his parents living just two houses away. It was over a year later when this all happened and we were all getting on with our lives except Tim and his family. I was moving in with Maurice. The children were now talking to him but still didn't trust him and they were finally talking to each other. Marti had moved into her own place and Victor was getting ready for college. Tim was still holding on to the past. He told Victor that when my relationship with Maurice ended he would be there to pick up the pieces. Victor told him he would not let him within ten feet of me and that no way in hell would he ever let me get back together with his father. Even though Victor was living with his father, I believe deep down Victor knew the truth; he was just in denial and could not cope with it. He like any son was desperate to have a real dad, just like I was desperate for my "dream" marriage and family. As for Tim's family they just threw me away and hid from the truth. They could not and cannot accept responsibility for the actions caused by them and those of their son over the years. They continue to blame me for the divorce, Tim's financial difficulties and the children having little to do with them.

21. Guilt

Guilt! How do I stop living with such guilt from the past? Every time I talk to my daughter I end up crying because I feel so bad about their childhood, the walking on eggshells all the time, having the house clean when Tim walked in, the tension all the time. How I let them down and how bad they had it? I told Marti how she makes me feel. She says sometimes she plays on my guilt and does it on purpose to deliberately upset me but most times she doesn't mean to. Last time we talked I cried and felt bad and she was so careful with her words. I don't want her to have to tip toe around words. I want her to say what she feels. She and her brother lived a terrible life growing up. They are dealing with the after effects and will for the rest of their lives as I do. But, I believe we can recover. The guilt is with me every day. I want to take away the pain my children feel. I was the adult, I should have been able to help them but, I couldn't. I never realized how controlling Tim was before we got married. Wanting sex all the time, which led to me getting pregnant and having to move the wedding date up, doing what he wanted when he wanted. How do I take away their pain and my guilt? Yesterday was Victor's 21st birthday and I forgot to call him. I went over my mom's house and remembered I had to call, but when I got home I was upset. Sometimes, for no apparent reason, the depression seeps back in and takes over. I was feeling extremely low, so it slipped my mind. I have never missed their birthdays. I called him the next morning and he said it was all right and not to worry about it. But I still felt bad. I want to help protect them. People don't understand that because I failed in the past that now I have to keep trying to protect them and help them. How do I get past the wanting to protect them even though I know I can't? Marti is 23 and Victor is 21; while they are not babies, they have not had a fair life and still their lives are hard.

Dealing with the guilt, the realization of my being throughout all of the abuse, I realized this when I found my daughters diary, our notes to each other and when I had a bad night at work. I knew then that what I did was right; and the heavy burden on my shoulders, the abuse, guilt and all that I questioned was lifted. I had wondered if it was actually as bad as it was until I found Marti's diary. There it was in her words how horrific things were. I knew then that I wasn't losing my mind and I could put the doubt away. I now had the strength to go on and to live a new fulfilling life. The elimination of the guilt and confusion began to lessen with each word I wrote, sharing the traumatizing events that took place in our heartbroken and despairing lives.

I was able to write this letter to Tim once I knew how miserable things really were for those horrendous years. Now, I knew the truth and could finally be comforted by it because I knew without a doubt that the abuse did indeed take place for the three of us. I did not imagine the abuse and my mind could finally grasp hold of the hideous truth I so desperately needed. I now had the strength and courage to write to him what was in my heart without fear.

Tim,

There are many kinds of ways for people to be strong. You see me as a weak person, because I did not stick it out. Because your mom is still with your dad and I did not stay with you. Well I am sorry. But I am a very strong person. It took a lot of courage and strength to do what I did. Knowing your temper and your past for blowing up, yet I still faced you down. I came between you, a hammer and our son. I was protecting him from a fear of a long time. Knowing how mad you were at the time. Knowing someone could and would get hurt if something was not done. Yet I stood there not backing down, you getting madder and madder. Knowing at anytime you would blow. And you did. To have me hurt instead of our son. Yes I would do it again, like the many times I stepped in between you two. Tell me something. How many times did you agonize over the beatings you gave him, or the extra slap you would give him because I stepped in? Tell me. How many times did you agonize over the beating you gave him when he was four years old? Tim you left welts and black and blue marks all over his legs and butt. Well I agonized and cried dearly over that and over many, many things that you did to him.

You didn't even lift a finger when Marti ran away. You stayed in the house and didn't even show one sign of emotion that our daughter was so unhappy that she felt she had to run away. I was the one who went out after her, staying up till she was safe at your folks house. Going to talk to her again and again, letting **her know** that **I love her**.

You put me down and say I am not a good mother. I should get to know my son better. Well let me tell you something. You say they would not be doing the things they are because of the divorce or if we were still together. Well Tim, they pulled lots of things long ago. Many things were hidden from you to protect them. You think Marti has pulled some things now or since she has been in college. Sorry but she pulled lots of things. The night I came home from work to go to the hospital. She was in bed with someone and had another couple out in the family room in bed.

As for Victor, that hasn't changed. He has always given me a hard time. Why not, you always overruled what I said anyway. So why should he listen to me now. These things that are going on now are not only from the divorce, but stem from many years of abuse and turmoil.

I had a hard night at work last night. But it made me realize how strong I am and how I do not do things on a whim or take things lightly. For many years I agonized over our relationship and our family situation. It was not a good one, but was all I had and the only life I knew at the time. I never felt like a strong person or good at anything. *That is the way you made me feel.* But I was strong and didn't know it. For all those years I was fighting and fighting hard to keep the children safe, a roof over their head and food in their stomachs. You always had a complaint about whatever was done. Nothing was ever good enough. It was always you first then the rest of us.

Many times you said you would put the fear of God into them, and you did. For they feared you like nothing else. How many times we hid things from you. That is being strong. Not being a wimp. Do you know how many times they did something and I took the blame. Fear for them. That is strong and being protective. Knowing Victor would get the fist, a slap, and kick or told he was stupid. Knowing Marti would get bad mouthed and poked in the chest by you. I knew I would feel your wrath, and yet I proceeded to go on. All the time not knowing how strong I was getting until that day you threatened our son with the hammer. My strength grew that day to no bounds and burst out.

And I am still getting stronger all the time, dealing with all that has happened since then. Sure I feel guilty sometimes but it will go away. For I know that I too was under your thumb just like the children. And I know that what I did was what I knew was right and the best for the time. It is all in the past and cannot be changed. The only thing to do now is to learn from it and grow and become stronger even more.

You always complained about my sister. Telling me if I was like her you would throw me out. You would not put up with her getting mad at Rob and not talking to him. Her attitude was bad and you didn't like me hanging around with her. Many times you said, "Oh you must have been talking to your sister again." Well Tim you were worse. You would go months without talking to your father. And how long did you go without talking to Meg when you got mad at her. You even went away for over a week and didn't call me because you were mad at me. Many times you would give me the cold shoulder after a fight. When I went to your work with a cut finger, you didn't even care. All you said was I was another bad spot in your already bad day. Sure you had me follow you to the emergency room. Big deal, I had to ask for a hug. That was really showing you cared. Tim you didn't make me feel loved or wanted at all.

I realized all this because I made a mistake at work, because I am a hard worker and care about what I am doing. I don't take things lightly and make rash decisions. I think and think about things before doing them. Rehash and agonize over them until I know what is right. I know getting a divorce was right. How could a person stay in a marriage without love and full of fear? You keep saying it happened so quickly. Well it did not, for I felt sad for a long, long time. You blame Maurice, saying it is because of him. Well it is not his fault. It is your fault and your treatment of me, and our children that brought us to the divorce. How can you say you loved me and wanted to be with me forever when you did what you did to me in the bedroom? You always warned me not to belittle you. But you did it to me all the time. Even when you would be wrong about something you would never apologize for it.

You say I didn't give you any signs. Well you had all kinds of signs. You even said it yourself. When you would hug me you would feel cold. The children didn't do anything with you. Why do you think Marti went away to college? Not to get an education, but to get out of this house. We went to counseling it worked for a while then things got even worse.

Many times the children' especially Marti would talk about walking on eggshells all the time. Many people talked to you about your temper and your treatment of us. I tried to talk to you. But it fell on deaf ears. I was even put on medication for a while. Almost had a break down and was depressed for a long time. But still you didn't get it. So you see Tim, you did have lots of signs. You chose not to see them.

You continue to blame me, telling me I took everything from you. Well I did not. You destroyed it for yourself. Tim take a good look in the mirror, look deep down inside and you will see who and what the cause of this family falling apart was. You will see why the children are the way they are and it is not because of me for I did what I knew how. I gave and gave until I could give no more. I am not at their beck and call anymore and I am not under your control any longer. But they do know that I love them very much.

Samantha

When I wrote this letter to him it set me free of a lot of the questions I had, and the guilt that plagued me every day. Now I don't have to second-guess my actions because I know they were right for the times that these terrible things were happening. I am not perfect, long from it, but I do know that I love my children and did everything I could to protect them. He buried me deep into myself and it felt like I was always clawing my way out. Finally I don't know where it came from, but the strength was there and as my sons poem says there was light and love. But, even after the divorce he still wanted control.

22. Tim's Drinking

My daughter had moved into her own apartment a few miles away from us. She called one day distraught. He father was just arrested, because of her. During the separation Tim started drinking and drinking heavily. Marti had made arrangements with her father to visit because they needed to talk. Things between them had been very tense since the break up. They spent the day painting her apartment. They had a few beers and chatted while painting. She and her father were putting up the boarder on the walls when things started to escalate. Tim started to get really agitated and upset about something insignificant that was said. Marti like me knew his moods and was not going to argue so she asked him to leave. This sent him over the edge and quickly things exploded. He then picked up her phone and hurled it across the room at her all the while screaming at her. Apparently he had bought her a color TV set for the apartment and said since he paid for it he wanted it back. She said no that he gave it to her, it was a gift, and he could not take it. Tim's family was good for that. Over the years they had given us things for the house, a dresser for the children, an entertainment center and a couch. But when it came to the divorce they said they only loaned these things to us and wanted them back. I was totally blown away by this. We had those items for years, they were not on loan to us but given to us. The couch was given to both of us as a house warming gift, but his parents being the materialistic people that they are wanted it back. The child's dresser and the entertainment center were also given back. Tim had other ideas too. He wanted things that my family gave to us. No freaking way was he getting thing from my side. I could pull the same thing he did, even though my therapist had said many times, not to play his games. The items he wanted were things that my twin brother had hand made and meant a lot to me. Why should his family want anything that was from my side, they had thrown me away without a questioning word as to what happened? They were only concerned with their standing in the family and community. Oh my, we are the first family to have a divorce. The divorce was an embarrassment, not to mention the blur it put on their social standings. Marti and Tim continued to argue; he then picked up the TV set and tore the plug out of the wall. She was yelling and screaming at him to stop but he was again out of control. He said she pushed him, but he tripped on the couch as he walked out the door with her TV set. Apparently he went home and got totally smashed after their altercation. She was hysterical and called her boyfriend and told him what happened. Marti thought Timothy was the only person she could count on; the one she could talk to about the constant strain she was under, because of the divorce and tempers that constantly flared up. This was the last straw. Evidently Timothy was tired of Marti crying all the time and always being emotionally wiped out because of her father. Marti's boyfriend, Timothy, called the police to have Tim, her father, arrested for domestic abuse. Marti had to go to the police station where she was asked to file a complaint against her father, so he could be arrested. She did not want to. After everything he had done to her, she still didn't want to have him put in jail. Tim was still her dad no matter what kind of monster he was. But, because a call had been made concerning domestic violence the police made out the report and Tim was arrested without Marti filing the complaint. At the police station Marti was given back the TV set.

Marti's grandparents were at the station also furious with her because their son had been arrested. His parents had to bail him out and were blaming the entire situation on Marti. Her grandmother said how dare she pull a stunt like that. It was a family matter and should be kept in the family. Then her grandmother told her she was no longer her granddaughter and was not welcome in their house anymore. Typical, none of them could ever take responsibility for their actions or acknowledge the abuse taking place.

By the time Victor moved in with his father, Tim had been drinking heavily. He got picked up for drunk driving once that I know of. One day my son had to call his Uncle Moe to pick him up, because his father was so drunk he was out of control and threatening him. Uncle Moe was not home but Jan was so she picked him up. Victor stayed with Jan for quite a while. Victor's grandmother kept calling and wanting to talk to him. Jan said she was being really nasty and rude on the phone. Jan told her that if she could not be nice then she would not be allowed to speak with Victor. He had enough emotional traumas and he didn't need to deal with a discourteous and disrespectful person. After all the years of biting her tongue and looking the other way, Jan was finally having her say. I was told that Uncle Moe went over to talk to Tim later that night. Tim was completely intoxicated and did not want to listen to reason. Moe was upset with Tim because of his behavior, his drunkenness and his threats to Victor. Moe never told anyone what happened that night. All we know is that Tim told him to get the hell out and not come back.

On another occasion, Victor arrived home late after work. He had called his father to let him know he would be a little later than expected. He and a buddy were going out to mess around and hang out after work. He was about a half - hour later than he said. His father was waiting for him and started yelling at him as soon as he walked in the door. Tim was intoxicated again. Victor told him to stop, that he didn't want to fight and he was going to go for a walk. He had learned to walk away from the situation before it got out of control. He had taken off his shoes at the door and was trying to put them back on, but his father would not let him have them. Tim kept shouting at Victor while trying to push him around. Victor then grabbed his father by the throat; in that instant, he said, everything came flooding back to him, all the years of abuse, the beatings, turmoil and anguish, he then told his father to back off "dad I don't want to fight with you." "We need to calm down now let me go." But his father, in his inebriated state, would not leave him alone. He kept pushing at him and hollering and being cruel to him. Victor had enough and he lost his temper. He pushed his father sending him tumbling over the trash barrel, which landed him on the floor. Victor then picked up a solid wooden chair and slammed it to the floor. *Crash* it shattered into bits and pieces sending splinters of wood everywhere. Tim thought he would get back at him and called the police. He thought he would teach Victor a lesson by having him arrested. He told the police that Victor tried to hit him with the chair. The police didn't believe it. There were no marks on him and Tim also had two prior arrests for drunkenness. But, what was a shocker to Tim was they both got arrested. Tim had thrown the first punch; it was domestic violence and both parties get arrested and are at fault. Because of the arrest they had to go to court. Uncle Moe and I went with Victor and Tim went with his parents. Tim and his parents sat on one side of the room while Victor, Uncle Moe and I sat on the other side of the room. No one said much to the other everyone was just plain mad, irritated with each other and upset about the situation at hand. After we entered the courtroom they both stood there hands clasped behind their backs looking at the judge. He lectured them telling them that they had to learn to get along and they both had to take anger management classes. We all left the courtroom together and went outside. Victor and his father hugged each other. Then Victor pushed me towards his father. He wanted me to hug him. I froze. No way, instant fear filled me. His father sensed my apprehension and said if and when the time was right, then he would get a hug. Victor still had some small hope, conscious or not, that his family would someday get back together. I then hugged Mr. D and told him I stilled loved him. He gave me a big hug and said he loved me back. Mrs. D on the other hand when I hugged her it was like hugging a cold steel pole. No emotion, just an icy glare coming from her bitter eyes. Tim called me a few days later and said he wanted me to pay for half of the anger management classes. He felt that because I had to pay for half of Victor's medical bills that I should have to pay for have of these classes too. I told him no, that this was not medical and it was his fault because of *his temper* and *his booze*. He was the one who had been drinking and would not let Victor leave the situation when he wanted to. He was also the one that called the police. It was his fault and he needed to take responsibility for his own actions.

A year later my son finally went away to school. I was glad he was away from his father. He didn't need to be around someone who was drunk all the time and was prone to abusive rages. His sister had moved to Connecticut to get away from her father and the family that had thrown her away.

23. *Phone Calls*

The now ex-in-laws never talked to me so I was shocked one day when Mrs. D left a message for me on the answering machine. So begins my emotional and confused thoughts of what was still transpiring, the heart breaking phone calls and the continued devastation of our lives.

May 1, 2003

What a day, May is supposed to be such a good month, warm weather, flowers and lots of sunshine. Not today, even years later, though all those things were occurring outside there are great dark clouds that shadow my children and me still. I don't think it will ever go away. I got a message on my answering machine from Mrs. D. She said that I know she would never call me unless it was a real emergency. Said Marti is in a bad way. She broke up with her boyfriend and her Uncle Moe is gone. She has no one to talk to and her cockroach boyfriend, Timothy that keeps using her is playing mind games with her. He constantly upsets her to the point that she cries all the time. I had realized a while back that Marti gravitated to someone very like her father. Mrs. D was afraid Marti would hurt herself; she even insinuated that I didn't keep in enough contact with my daughter. A lot she knows. When I called Marti to see if she was okay she was trying to sleep. I asked how she was and she told me not okay I asked why and she didn't want to talk. I kept encouraging her, letting her know if she wanted to talk I was there for her. She said she didn't want to get upset again. I asked if it had anything to do with Timothy. She yelled at me and got upset, said yes, and said she had to go. So today May 1, later she called me to apologize for going off on me. She told me that Timothy was in Florida with someone else. She told me that the beginning of the week he was talking about getting her an engagement ring. He text messaged her phone and called her stupid because he was there earning extra money for her ring. He then told her she was being psycho again. Marti, like me, has been diagnosed with *Post Traumatic Stress Disorder and has also been diagnosed as a Manic Depressive person*. She tried calling the airlines, the Florida police and Timothy's hotel. She doesn't trust him at all. He uses her for money and sex, but she doesn't see it. She sees only that he was there when her father and I were going through the divorce. She says that he is her lifeline. She doesn't see how she is every time she is with him; upset all the time, crying, yelling at me, more depressed, and more in debt. She is so happy without him, so very much in denial. I talked to my therapist about it. She says that she never got the love and attention from her father, so she will get it from someone like him. I guess so. Her father name is Tim, with abusive ways and the guy she is seeing is also Timothy with the same abusive traits.

Marti also told me on the phone that she finally blew up at her grandmother. She told her they never did anything to help all those years of abuse and turmoil. Mrs. D said blood is thicker than water. Marti really lost it then. She said, "What the hell are she and Victor? We are your blood, we are your god damn grandchildren and you did nothing to help. When my Timothy called the cops on dad you threw me away blaming everything on me. You said it was a family matter and he should not have gotten involved." Marti told her grandmother that it was about time someone called the cops on her father. For if it had been done years ago, she and Victor would not have gone through all the physical and mental abuse and mom would not have gone through the sexual abuse as well. Mrs. D. told Marti that she was lying. She had never heard anything about the sexual abuse. Of course not, why would I tell of such a shameful thing? To me I could handle that better than my children could handle their abuse. I would keep my hideous secret locked away from everyone; my children were dealing with enough. Why would Tim ever tell his mother of the sexual abuse he caused? She told Marti I was making it up about the sexual abuse. Marti let her have the bomb and told her to ask her son about it, because she certainly was not going to believe Marti. Marti also told her he is the one that relayed the information about the sexual abuse to her and not me. Mrs. D couldn't say anything. She must have had to really eat crow to leave that message on my answering machine. Marti then told me she is back on anti-depressants and that she has thought about hurting herself. She said the pain would all go away. I am so afraid for her. I told her to call me anytime especially after she hears from Timothy. I know she will be upset if he doesn't have a ring for her. She doesn't have insurance so medical help is hard for her. I can't put her on my policy because she isn't in school and doesn't live with me. Otherwise I would. I told her to check into clinics. A good thing she told me is that her GYN is giving her free birth control. She told me about her gaining weight and continued drinking. Told me how everyone looks down on her for her life because she didn't finish college or go into the service, become a nurse or something better. All I could do was tell her I never did that and I told her I love her no matter what. Told her I love her and we said good-bye. Timothy did bring her back a ring. She was so excited when she called to tell me. But how could I be truly happy for her when I could see the true situation. He is disrespectful to her and judgmental of her. It's like living with her father all over again. What exists between them in my eyes is fighting and hollering all the time. He ridicules, belittles and has abusive tendencies, but again, Marti is in denial.

Marti's father has been in Iraq for the last few months. He will be coming home soon. She will not go meet him. She is afraid of what he will say and do or how he will be when he finds out that she has been seeing Timothy again and what he has been putting her through. Marti said she would go over another time when all the Dudleys are not around. Marti is on a constant emotional roller coaster. Such phone calls always upset me terribly, so when I went over my mom's as I always do on Friday it was with a heavy heart, chest pains and not able to breathe all this because of one controlling person, her father. Most times I would feel guilty about my children, but not on this day. I think it is because everything is coming out and I know that what she is doing is from the lack of love and affection from her father. Again I talked to Marti; we were on the phone for four hours this day going over what happened in the past and what continues to happen now seven years later. She called her grandmother to talk. Again Marti asked her why she didn't help them out. This time the blame was all mine. Mrs. D said help was never given, because I told her to stay out of it because it would only make matters worse for us. Marti tried to explain to her how terrified I was because of Tim's threats to me all the time. He would constantly threaten to take the children away from me so the only choice I had was to have people stay out of our business and our house of horror. Her grandmother told Marti that she would always side with her son and she would have helped him take the children away from me even though she knew what was going on in the house. And again stating blood is thicker than water. But she had always told me that she would be there for the children and me but again she denies the truth of the situation and that her son was, and still is, a very abusive controlling person. Mrs. D still blames Maurice for the divorce saying, I was cheating on Tim and that is why I divorced him. Also, she says she is still angry with me for taking him to the cleaners. She is in complete denial of the situation and only has Tim's side of the facts. Everything was split down the middle. Both lawyers made sure of that and I agreed not to touch his pension or 401K plans in return to stay in the house, which was offered to him to begin with. Mrs. D said I lied about everything. When I said it was the lawyers she said that I should have spoken up. Maybe I should have spoken up with all the facts that took place. Because the judge would have been completely horrified as to what took place in our house for so many years. Mrs. D doesn't realize that I begged my lawyer not to bring up the abuse because it would have been too hard for my children to go through again and at the time I didn't want it to become public. She still has never talked to me about the divorce and the circumstances, which took place leading up to that day.

Marti mentioned how Victor keeps stating that he wants to change his name. That he no longer wants to be a Dudley because of all that keeps occurring over time. For the first time Marti said the same thing to me in our four hour conversation. Evidently she mentioned it to her grandmother and Mrs. D said, "If Victor wants to change his name then he has my blessings. If it embarrasses him and makes him feel like a hypocrite then he should change it. Then he would no longer be associated with their family and could stay out of their lives." Then her grandmother told her to just get over it all and stop bringing it up that it was a long time ago. Marti said, "How can I just forget 19 years of abuse, it isn't that easy especially when everyone keeps judging me." It is in her being and she still has nightmares because of the abuse and still carries a lot of guilt around that should not be hers to carry.

Marti told me how she used to play magic or go for rides to the moon when she was grounded in her room to pass the time. She would use her video chair as the cockpit of her space ship on her travels to the moon.

Her stuffed animals were the passengers on the trips. Marti told me how she would crawl under her bed and make believe that was her magic room where she kept all her potions. She had little bottles on the rails under her bed filled with love potions, powders, dust and such for her to use. She recalled the times I would sneak in a sandwich to her because she was sent to her room without supper. Marti said she knew it was always something thrown together quickly so we would not get into trouble. A peanut butter and jelly sandwich, crackers and bread with butter on it were a few things brought into the children, so their little tummies would not rumble. We talked about the parties we would have when her father was away. Her sixteen-birthday party was a blast. She was allowed to invite 20 friends for the afternoon but about 50 kids showed up throughout the day. There were baby pictures of her and baby clothes that she wore hung on the doors. There were all kinds of food and drink for the kids to eat and plenty of music for them to listen to. A few of her friends even tried to throw me into the pool but when I glared at them they decided differently. Marti always had friends around her and went to many functions at school. When she told me that she was so lonely and had no real friends in school it broke my heart. She mentioned her trip to the Beach in high school. I thought she had a splendid time, but she did not. Marti told me how she had no one to room with and had to be put on the extra persons list. She had no one to hang around with either. She went on the rides by herself and even tried to hang out with the teachers. Even they couldn't be bothered with her, she was so alone and unhappy keeping it all bottled up inside. Festering like a bad infection, just growing and growing without chance of a cure. Marti had become me, only younger. Marti had to protect her family secrets by hiding the deep dark pathetic ugliness that existed in her everyday life. She could not let it seep out for all to witness. Marti mentioned how we remember certain events differently. I always remember her not being around when her brother was getting beaten on, but she said that she was always there watching and wondering why she wasn't getting hit and pushed around. Marti even mentioned how she was glad it was her brother and not she, but that she would feel guilty for thinking like that. Once again I told her to give the guilt back to the person who did the abusing and who made all our lives a living hell. But Marti said it is easier said than done, and I agree with her. Nineteen years of abuse will not go away easily, if ever. Marti talked about her aunt and how she yells all the time and that her uncle drinks a lot. She said that Jay Jay is like her brother because of all the yelling. I told her that it was the same in our house because of the tension. All anyone knows over there is yelling and that is the same as we had. We took it out on each other all the time. We couldn't and didn't dare speak up to their father, because we knew we would once again feel his wrath. She recounted the many fights she had with her brother. The broken cabinet door, the glue on the floor, the fist fights, the scratching each other, the screaming and hollering at each other just to state a few.

Then the topic, which was the hardest to talk about, came up and that is the sexual abuse by her father. When she was younger she had to get something for her father out of his dresser drawer. Upon going into the drawer she found a dildo he had hidden there. She didn't know what it was at the time; she only knew it felt slimy. She put it back never saying a word to anyone about it. Marti remembers all the times that she and her brother were not allowed into the family room because her father would be taping dirty videos all day long. She forgot one day and went into the family room. She was screamed at for going into the room by her father and told to get the hell out of the room on the double. His end table was full of dirty magazines and videos and creams. We talked about sex and I told her that it was the first time a few weeks earlier that I was actually able to say to myself, and admit that her father raped me up the ass. He often said that anal and oral sex was intimate, but it was not. She and I agreed that it could be if both persons agree on it and if it does not hurt the other person. Marti again said how disgusted she was with her father for that and that she gets very uncomfortable when he hugs her. She mentioned again how embarrassed she was when her father got an erection when he checked out her best friend Rachel's tattoo. Marti told me how selfish I was once I was free from her father. I agreed with her totally. I was free for the first time in 19 years and I was going to enjoy every minute of that freedom. I also wanted what was mine and that meant the car she was using. I was given the car as part of the divorce settlement. Marti was allowed the use of the station wagon pretty much as she wanted after her father left. She went anywhere and everywhere with the car. It was her wheels to and from school and to visit Timothy. I arrived at school one day and told her I was tired of hers lies about the use and whereabouts of the car and was taking it back. The car was to be sold, so I could pay the lawyer and bills that accrued during the divorce proceedings. Marti had not been told that her father and I had separated when she was home for the holidays. We felt at the time it was better that she didn't know because of the amount of pressure she was under being away at school. After taking the car, Marti felt she didn't have her own means of transportation to and from school. She felt that she was dumped at school during the time leading up to the divorce. She felt betrayed, left out, discarded and neglected. She felt that it was not fair that she was left at school with no one to talk to and no way to escape the devastation of being alone. Marti felt that Timothy was her only salvation and now she had no way to get to him. Marti also told me that I was selfish leaving Victor by himself all the time. Again I agreed with her. I told her that Victor and I talked about this period of time and he forgives me. She was also told that Victor relayed to me that his therapist said I had every right to be selfish for a while. Marti and I talk often and many subjects come up from our dreary past, which we are still dealing with. Marti is very emotional and has many mood swings many of which are not good.

On this day, when I called my brother, he informed me of a phone call Victor had with his father. He told me that my son had another argument with his father. Victor wants to get his remaining things out of his father's house. The argument escalated and the yelling started. Zoe, Victor's wife, even told Tim that he was an asshole. She has lost all respect for her father-in-law and wants nothing more to do with him. Tim told Victor that he could not have his things unless he paid back all the monies he owes him, which the amount keeps conveniently going up every time Victor talks to him. Victor ended up calling Maurice and asking for the lawyer's number that I used in the divorce. He is totally fed up with his father and again mentioned that he wants to change his name. Tim keeps saying how much he has changed, but his actions still show otherwise. Unfortunately, even after all the years that have passed, the children continue still with the controlling ways of their father.

24. *New Directions*

Maurice and I were married in July of 2002. I was upset that my son would not be able to attend the wedding. He was still in Oklahoma at school and could not afford to come home. It was the night of the rehearsal. We were standing outside the hall when Uncle Moe drove up in his truck. I thought it was so nice that he show up for me. But when I looked in the truck it was not Uncle Moe; it was my son. Maurice and my daughter had made plans to fly him home to surprise me and they certainly did. Victor was barely out of the truck when I opened the door and hugged him and cried my eyes out. I was so happy to see him. Our wedding day was a great day for me. It meant so much to me that my family, friends and my children were accepting Maurice into the family. My son told me he now had three fathers, his father the controlling person, Uncle Moe the trouble - maker (but in the fun sense) and Maurice the logical father. Victor would call from school and talk to Maurice to get advice, because he knew Maurice would not laugh at him, would not judge him and would listen to him and he would not put him down like his own father would. My son mentioned after the wedding that his father said he would be there waiting for me when my marriage to Maurice fell apart. Again Victor told him that no way in hell would he let his father get within ten feet of me and that no way would he let the two of us get back together. We have all moved on, but his father is still stuck in the past hoping for what will certainly never be.

My son moved to Oklahoma to go to school for auto mechanics. He was there for approximately two years and that is where he met Zoe, now, his wife. What a nice girl. When they called and told me they were engaged I was thrilled. After the wedding they were planning on moving here to Massachusetts. I was ecstatic until, I found out that they were going to live with his father. I knew his father had not changed and there would be trouble, I still saw the signs in Tim's behavior. I told Victor it was a big mistake, but he insisted that his father had changed. Tim showed a very nice side of himself at the wedding. Victor's Uncle Moe could not be his best man, because he was serving time in Iraq, so he asked his father to stand up for him. Still trying to control the situation; Tim insisted that Maurice and I not be put at the same table with him. After all this time he was still trying to control my son and me. It didn't work out the way he planned; Maurice and I sat next to him during the meal. Though the tension was present; it went very well. Tim's family made no attempt to go to the wedding, but they insisted that Tim call them during the ceremony so they could hear it. Of course, he did, and through the entire ceremony the justice of the peace held Tim's cell phone up while they said their vows. I had tears in my eyes as I looked at my son, so handsome and grown up in his tux. I stood there watching him dance with his new wife feeling so very proud of him. Victor endured a lot of heartache, as well as physical abuse as a child; now the challenge of being an adult was ahead of him. I only hope and pray that the damage he endured for such a long period of time will be used as a positive tool for the future. I hope he learned from what his father did to him. And I believe he will deal with his own situations with a level head, an open heart, and a soft hand. It has always been a running joke that when I dance with someone much taller than me, they put a chair in the middle of the floor and I stand on it. When it came time for me to dance with my son, he did the same thing. After a minute of being on the chair he scooped me up and held me like a rag doll and danced around the floor. It was quite a site, Victor being over six feet tall and me only 4' 11" tall. Everyone started laughing. My head barely reached his chest after he let me slide down to touch the floor. I held up my hands about a foot apart indicating that he was only this big when he was born. It was such a glorious day. His dad gave a toast and said not to take his wife for granted and to treat her with a lot of respect and kindness. Maybe he did learn a little something because of his abusive behavior. When, as the result of his poor decisions and abusiveness, he lost his family as he once knew it.

The next day we showed up at the kid's place to spend a little time with them before leaving for home that evening. Tim was there when we arrived and was civil to Maurice. What else could he do? He truly wanted the kids to see the charade side, the good side he was portraying. We ordered pizza and had a nice time. The children were married in August and moved to Massachusetts in September. No amount of talking could dissuade them from moving in with his father. Trepidation filled me; for I knew from the start that it would not go well. Past behaviors had not shown me that Tim had changed. For the first few weeks things went well. Slowly, as Zoe put it, Tim's true colors came out; the charade was over, the play-acting gone. Jekyll and Hyde was never gone. They would come over to visit and complain how demanding Tim was on Victor and how he persistently badgered him. Zoe was very upset by this and told me she could not believe the bad side of her new father-in-law she was seeing. He was so different in Oklahoma, he really hoodwinked everyone. Zoe said she spent a lot of time in her room in tears because of Tim. She did not want to listen to his constant demands upon Victor or listen to him degrade and humiliate her new husband. The entire time they stayed with him he made them pay a large rent, do chores and help pay for food; and of course nothing was ever up to his expectations. The kids would come over as often as they could. They couldn't stand being at the house with him. They could not even call it home, it was his domain and he let them know it each and every day. This one particular night they came over for supper because they had to get out of the house. The constant badgering was too much for them. Zoe wanted to play a game of dice. Victor and Marti used to play this game with me; Victor tried to show Zoe how to play, but could not remember the rules. We put in a video, Maurice fell asleep on the couch, Zoe and I were at the table playing dice and Victor went down cellar and brought up two large buckets of Lego bricks. Here was a married man; weighting about 275 pounds sitting on the floor playing with plastic bricks. Victor spent a lot of time playing by himself when he was little. I think that he missed so much of his child hood that he still needed to try and get some of it back when he could. He has always been good with his younger cousins and would always play with them and get down to their level. I looked at him sitting there and my heart went out to him. Again guilt came back to me, but not because of what I was unable to give him as a child growing up in a world of despair, but because of what his father robbed him of for so many horrific years. Zoe and I just looked at him. With a big smile; I turned to my daughter-in-law and said he would be a great daddy because he would not be afraid and it would not bother him to get down on the floor and play with his children. I call my son the *gentle giant*, he is so big and strong; but there is also a surging amount of gentleness to him you can easily see when you look at him. A *miracle*, after all he endured. My son admitted to me that I was right and they should not have moved in with his father. It caused a lot of heartache and misery; his father still trying to be in control and very demanding of them.

It was a Sunday night, when Victor and Zoe came to visit. Usually I am in bed by three in the afternoon, so I can get sleep before going into work at 11 pm. But, I had been out of work because of surgery on my foot. They had gone to a family day celebration at the base with his father and the Dudleys the day before and were talking about it. From what they told me, the Dudleys had been involved with support groups for families of service men overseas. They got an award for family support; how ironic. When Victor told me this I laughed and walked away. I went into the kitchen to get a drink. He came in and asked what was up? I told him I wasn't getting into that conversation, but he kept asking me, so I told him. What a joke that they got an award for family support. He said why? I said "Where the hell were they when you were little? When you and your sister were going through all that shit from your father? They always told me that they would be there for us. When it came down to it they just threw me away. Every time your sister spoke her mind or someone stuck up for her, because your father was being a jerk again, they would throw her away over and over again." Then I said, "drop it; subject done and over with." I could feel the resentment towards them building. I could feel myself getting angrier as we spoke and knew it was time to walk away.

The future for Marti is still unclear. Her mood swings and depression are still a constant battle. Marti called and said she was getting evicted. She had wanted to borrow money from me, but I hadn't worked in a month so I couldn't help her. She called again the next day and was furious with me. I told her brother about her problem and he blabbed to everyone. He told their father - who told his parents - who keep throwing Marti away. She asked me not to tell her brother anything again because she doesn't need to hear it from everyone how she is just a waste and using everyone. Marti had a few student loans, which she couldn't pay back. Her father is paying for one of them and her aunt is paying another. Marti was paying on it and let it lapse, so the Dudleys finally had to pay off the balance of her loan. Marti was young and naive when she went to college. She charged up credit cards and bounced checks; so her credit is bad. Now she can't have a checking account. The worst part of this is that she believes her Timothy has about 50, 000 dollars sitting in the bank from an inheritance. I told her to ask him for help. They are engaged and living together. If she is out of the apartment so is he. He said he would not help. He says the money is for a home someday. She has, as I did, found someone, who is always first on his agenda. He has lived with Marti for seven years with minimal contribution to their lives! Marti called a few days later and said she got the money for the rent and not to worry. Told me not to tell her brother anything or she would not confide in me again. I have to keep the communication open with her; she talks crazy sometimes and wants it all to end. She and Timothy came to visit one day shortly after that altercation. She had been in an accident and wanted to see me. We were sitting at the table and Timothy was watching the news about the hurricane that was coming. Marti got up and went to look at a picture my brother had made me; it was on top of the entertainment center. She got in front of the TV set and I couldn't believe what happened next. Timothy said "Hey stupid get out of the way." She moved like it was nothing. I looked at him and tapped his arm and told him not to ever talk to her like that again. We visited a little longer and they went to leave. He should have helped her down the stairs with her leg in a cast, but he didn't.

They had come over in his Cameo, nice car. First time I had seen it so I wanted to sit in it. Timothy was in the driver's side and I sat in the passenger's side. I could barely see over the dash because the car is so low to the ground. Timothy made a smart remark about me being short. I told him to stop being a smart ass and to behave. You would think that he would show respect knowing he was already on the shit list. I believe he should know enough to show respect for his future mother in law. Everything is all about him; he is so much like her father. The therapist says that because she didn't get love from her father, she needs to find that love and will be drawn to the same miserable abusive type of guy her father is. But, Marti denies it and says Timothy is nothing like her father. Each time I would see the doctor he would ask about both children especial Marti. His concerns for her are great. Each time he would say to me that Marti is again in denial of what took place for so many traumatizing years and that the men in her life are a reflection of what she endured in the past. She seeks the abusing sort of man because that is what she relates to. Her relationships will constantly be a battle field for her with many storms to overcome and until she comes to terms with what she was dealt as a child; she will always be looking for approval from men like her father. Marti is very emotional all the time, she is very angry with her father and grandparents especially when they tell her to just get over it and forget it. It is not so easily done. She is a manically depressed person and that can easily escalate out of control. For her it can simply be triggered by the smallest recollection or event that occurred years ago. Marti and Timothy are no longer engaged. They still see each other, but the road is extremely stormy for them. Marti feels Timothy is her lifeline and that he was the only one there for her during the divorce. She is beginning to see his faults and the fact that he uses her all the time, but still she hold on to the hope that they will someday be together always.

25. *Kids' Troubles*

It was Victor and Zoe's first Christmas as a married couple; so they wanted to put up a tree and decorations. Tim was adamant and said, "no way." They could not put up a tree or any decorations whatsoever. Tim had, since the divorce been playing poor me. His claim, he still hurt too much because the separation took place around the holidays. This was a few years later and he was still playing "feel sorry for me." I lost everything look at me I can't stand Christmas look what she did to me." His family would even complain about me during meals. On Thanksgiving they were putting me down yet again in front of my daughter. This time she went *ballistic* and told them to stop putting me down and that the situation at hand was not my fault. Of course they got mad at her for speaking out against their son, but they forgot that her father was not the victim; we were. He is the one that abused us physically and mentally with all the hollering, beatings and bruising. They are so unyielding in their denial of the circumstances that took place for so many horrendous years.

None of the relatives went to Victor's wedding in Oklahoma except for his father, Maurice and me. The Dudleys kept saying they were going to have a reception for the kids when they moved to Massachusetts, but that I was not invited. Zoe said she did not want another ceremony because she married Victor once and that was the day she would always remember. They never gave the kids a reception; on their first anniversary I decided to give them a big party. We decided on a Hawaiian theme and planned the party. Zoe's mom and best friend flew in from Oklahoma to surprise her for the party. Maurice and I live in a condo complex so we rented the community room, attached to the pool house. There is an indoor pool, steam room and hot tub in the pool house. There was lots of delicious food to eat, plenty to drink and music to dance to. Through tear filled eyes and cracking voice my daughter made a toast to her brother and his wife. She and her brother now get along and know that they really do love each other even though they still argue. We had a marvelous time. We played volleyball in the pool for hours, listened to music and ate lots of food. Victor and Zoe opened many gifts making the day a complete success. Maurice family joined us for the festivities and it is, hopefully, clear to Victor and Zoe, that they have an extended family that will never throw them away. But the Dudleys, being the controlling people they are, let it be known that they were unhappy with me because I had the party without consulting them. They wanted to be involved in the party and wanted a say in what was to take place. I told Victor to let his father know that I didn't want any trouble on their special day. It was well known they didn't want anything to do with me, so I had a party everyone could enjoy.

Victor and Zoe call me and tell me that Tim wants the money they owe him. They are young and just starting out, but he wants what is his and that is that. He told Victor that he had to pay for the truck that his father gave to him as a graduation gift. When he turned 21 he was supposed to get the 1971 Ford pickup truck. It was in the divorce agreement. Victor decided that he didn't want to take the chance that something would happen to the truck while he was in Oklahoma. His father wouldn't be able to hold it over his head if something happened to the precious black truck so he decided to take the 1991 red truck instead. Victor told his father "okay you want money then I want the black truck, it is legally mine in the divorce agreement." They had a huge disagreement which; ended up with them not talking to each other for months (Gee, sounds just like Tim and his dad). Not only that, but Victor's grandmother called and started yelling at him. He told her they liked material things and mentioned about the entertainment center, couch and the money she gave him for school. She had given him money for school and told him not to worry about paying it back. Now because she was mad she wanted him to pay back the money. They had words on the phone and she told her grandson to go to hell. In my opinion, it doesn't matter how upset you are at your grandchildren; you are the adult and you don't keep throwing them away and don't tell them to go to hell. Every time there was a family function Victor and Zoe would go for just a short while; they always felt uncomfortable. I was invited to my godson's confirmation; I was shocked that someone was actually standing up to the Dudleys' controlling ways. Zoe and I went together, Victor had to work. The first thing out of his grandmother's mouth was not, hi Zoe how are you? But, "My grandson must still be mad at me." Zoe had been feeling so uncomfortable because of all the tension and arguing going on that she left with me right after pictures were taken.

26. *Annulment*

Tim and I were married 19 years and had been divorced for five years when to my astonishment a letter arrived in the mail from the Diocese of Springfield, The Tribunal. Tim was trying to have our 19-year marriage annulled, invalidated. He wants to be able to get married in the church again and has now petitioned for a religious invalidation of our marriage. It took me completely by surprise when the notice was received in February of 2003. After everything that has happened he is still trying to have control and the last word. A lot of questionnaires went out to friends and family members on what they felt the status of the marriage was and what they felt his treatment of us was. The annulment is something that should not happen. Yes, over the years I have said many times that I wish I had my children without their father. At least they would have had a decent childhood and would have happy memories from it. But instead they are still dealing with the after affects from a very abusive situation, emotional ups and downs, anger, hatred and scaring that will last a lifetime. In May of 2003 I was notified that the appeal was to go forward. At this time a 26-page questionnaire was filled out and sent to the tribunal along with many pages of journal entries that were made throughout the years since the divorce. Two years later, in January of 2005, the Tribunal notified me that a decision had been made; but that it had to go through the Appeals Court, which would then render the final decision. The letter also stated that I had approximately 20 days to lodge a personal appeal challenging the decision of the Tribunal. I was greatly surprised by these findings since I had not received any further information pertaining to this matter. After four letters of appeals to the Archdiocese of Boston, in July of 2005 the Metropolitan Tribunal confirmed the final decision.

"On May 6, 2003 you lodged an appeal against the affirmative decision given by the Diocesan Tribunal of Springfield. The Metropolitan Tribunal of the Archdiocese of Boston, as the Court of Second Instances, contacted you on June 14, 2005 inviting you to give testimony in support of your appeal. Taking into full account the further observations, which you have offered, the Metropolitan Tribunal proceeded to adjudicate the case according to the norm of law. On July 22, 2005 the college of three Judges issued a second affirmative decision, declaring your marriage to Tim Dudley to be invalid."

Ironically enough the letter arrived on Maurice and my third wedding anniversary. We were on our way to dinner to celebrate and stopped to get the mail. I was deeply upset with the findings and threw the letter on the floor of the car along with my keys and started to cry. I just didn't understand after all that had been documented and forthcoming; how the church could let this man get married in the church again and wreak havoc on another unsuspecting victim. The wretchedness, being high-strung, and abusiveness was all still part of Tim's personality. How could the church just clean the slate of years of such behavior? The depression, flashbacks, emotional ups and downs and nightmares all still exist in each of us. Now he would be free to bully and control yet another trusting and innocent person as if nothing he ever did to us mattered or took place.

Maurice calmed me down and said to call or write a letter if I was still unclear on the understanding of how the appeal court works and that of its findings. The next day I sent another letter to the appeals court in hope of finding some answers to my many questions. Three weeks later I talked to Father Bradley and he explained how the court reached its judgment. First Tim had to apply for the invalidation through the church. Then a petition had to be set into motion for an investigation to begin concerning the case at hand, Dudley vs. Dudley; should the marriage have taken place in the first place. After taking into account all information given the court, the Springfield Tribunal reached its first decision on invalidation. Then the case was sent to the Metropolitan Tribunal to adjudicate in the norm of the law. The second invalidation was the resolution by the tribunal. The finding of the tribunal, and, ultimately, the reason for the invalidation of the marriage, was that Tim was not stable at the time of the marriage, nor was he capable of acting responsibly throughout the marriage. The questionnaires show both sides of the family, his and mine agreed on his behavior, which was extremely abusive and controlling from the start of the relationship, and in some instances even before the marriage took place. Father Bradley also explained that even though Tim thought he was mature enough to be married, he really was not. The court found that he was incapable of acting in the best interest of the family and was not able to carry out his functions as a husband and father throughout the marriage. He also said that in some cases like this one which was very abusive from the beginning, that a block will be placed on the abusive individual so he or she cannot be married again until said person shows that they have gone through counseling and have been deemed fit to remarry. Father Bradley also stated that Tim was totally surprised by my actions for the divorce. He explained that Tim is still incapable of taking responsibility for his actions and that denial is a great source of comfort. The investigation shows that everything I was capable and competent of doing was done on my part to keep the marriage whole and to try and protect the children. Tim's abusive ways, controlling manner and instability were detrimental to the marriage and ultimately caused it to dissolve.

27. Still Paying the Price

My daughter feels most of the effects at the holidays but she is stronger now. Marti has gone to counseling, which has helped tremendously, although she stops when the counselor starts getting close to her real feelings. She is scared and has a lot bottled up. She says the closer she gets to remembering things, she cracks and can't do it. She is so terrified of what she will recall and doesn't want to go through the misery, despair, anger and hurt all over again. When she gets home after a session, she is completely drained emotionally and physically for the rest of the day. She told me that her counselor thinks that her father may have touched her inappropriately and that she has suppressed it completely. I knew nothing of this, just as I didn't know he would make her pull down her pants and lie on the bed while he whipped her with the belt as a punishment when she did something wrong.

One traumatic episode, for example, occurred when Marti was about 12 or 13 years old. After having gotten into trouble, she went into her bedroom and assumed the position; that is, she pulled her pants down and lay across the bed. Marti told me that her father was livid with what he saw when he entered the room. He told her to pull up her pants, and left the room. When her father went back into the room, he started blaming Marti for exposing herself to him - she was completely humiliated by this.

She was only preparing herself to be spanked in the way that had been expected of her for as long as she could remember. He screamed at her for doing exactly what she had grown up with, *and then whipped her just the same*. She is afraid to have children because of her emotional distress. She doesn't know what will come up to haunt her as she grows older and is utterly afraid to face her demons. When Marti was told about this book she said she would be incapable of reading it. She could not bear to read the hurt and go through it all again. Even after all these years Marti is still afraid and uncomfortable to hug her father. Again she mentioned how it sickens her to have him touch her after finding out that he sexually abused me. Marti stated again how humiliated, mortified and embarrassed she was when her father got an erection from looking at the tattoo on her friends shoulder. We each have so much pain, each of us with so many terrible secrets, no one to trust and no one to turn to. The terrible things that are locked away in my mind, no wonder I still have so many horrible nightmares. Marti had a conversation with her father about his behavior throughout the years. He said that they didn't have it so bad; "I didn't beat you into a bloody pulp and land you in the hospital." So this makes it okay!

By Tim's own writing to me when we first separated he said, *"Every time I hit Victor it comes back and haunts me, every time I yelled at him for no reason it comes back to haunt me. I lie awake in bed and relive every time it happened. Believe me when I tell you I know I have a problem and it hits me every night. I know a lot of people have told me over and over that I need help, I should have listened but I didn't, I was an idiot for not listening."* From another letter he wrote to me again early in the separation he said, *"There is one thing I want you to know and that is that I have realized that you are a strong woman to do what you did. I've realized that you had to do it because things would have only **gotten worse** and that it took a lot to stand up to me. I also realize that it hasn't been easy for you since I left. Samantha don't ever doubt yourself on this one, you **did the right thing** for both you and the children."* Tim wrote good letters, said all the right things that I wanted and needed to hear. However, when we came face to face he was still in denial of the events that occurred by his own hand. His temper would flare and I would get yelled at, and with each day he didn't get his way his abusiveness would become apparent.

Tim still can't or is unwilling to except responsibility for what he did. Marti also told me of a conversation with her grandmother. She again asked why they didn't help us when she and her brother would go over crying and pleading for help because it was so unbearable. Marti's grandmother said, she didn't remember the children ever going over to her house crying and asking for help. It is documented in these pages all the times we cried out for help. Many times she saw the bruises on us and heard the hollering, screaming and the hitting that happened on a daily basis. I believe she is unable to come to terms with the fact that her son was and in my opinion is still an abusive person. When my mom called her after Tim and I first split up to talk to her about the circumstances she said to my mom, "He only hit her three times." Mom was furious with her and told her that he should not have hit me even one time. So many secrets still hidden so many occurrences still locked away all of us still trying to cope with a hideous past. Time and again I remember watching in fear, as he would beat on my son. But Marti told me differently; ***over and over again I didn't just stand watching***. She remembers many; many times I would throw myself on top of Victor to protect him. Tim would literally shove me out of the way and go on with striking her brother. Marti told me there were times she would scream at her father to try and divert his attention. Come on dad hit me. She was daddy's girl and thought back then that he would not hit her, but it didn't work. He would ignore both our pleas and inflict more of the same cruelness upon Victor. She also told me how crushed she was the day I slapped her face. Marti said it was the one and only time I hit her. She had been mouthing off dreadfully to me and I was quite fed up with it and slapped her. Marti said it devastated her so much, because I never hit them. Her father always hit them. She knew she could count on me not to hit her. I broke what trust she had in me when I struck her. Little things come back to Marti each time we talk. One such story is when she had to go back to school for a book she had forgotten. She was not allowed to use the car but did just the same. When her father got home of course he asked her if she did use the car. Marti being terrified as always denied using it. When her father went out to the garage to change the oil in the car it was still warm. He then asked her again and told her that he would not get angry with her if she told the truth. She then admitted taking the car and of course he got quite upset with her and grounded her once again. Marti believes that because I was standing there, she didn't feel his wrath quite so severely.

Another story she told about was when she was a little girl in elementary school. She brought home an ornament from school to put on the Christmas tree. He father told her not to place it on the tree yet. That she should wait for me to get home. I was due home shortly from work. Marti being small and excited couldn't wait and put the ornament on the tree before I arrived. She wanted it on the tree to show me her own shining work of art. She remembers her special decoration staying on a shelf throughout the holidays. Her father got mad at her for putting the decoration on the tree without waiting for me. He took it off the tree, placed it on the shelf and that is where it stayed until we packed it away with the rest of the Christmas decorations. She also told me how devastated she was when her father told her there was no Santa Claus. He sat her on the step to the garage and told her Santa was not real. Marti said she thought it was the end of the world. I took my daughter into my arms and held her tight as she cried. I couldn't believe he could be so cold-hearted to tell that beautiful little girl just a few short days before Christmas the there wasn't a Santa Claus. Marti said she hated that step. So many times she was told to sit there and would get scolded for something. She also remembers watching her brother cower in the corner of the garage from that step. He had been either threatened by his father, or told to hold something that was extremely heavy for a small boy to keep in his grasp. When she was little she would walk home from school. Her father would get out of work at 3 o'clock and be home by 3:30. On her way back from school she would have to pass the house. Tim would be out in the garage working on one of the vehicles. Marti would get excited to see him and want to go home. Tim would scold her and tell her to get her butt to the babysitter's house. He would not pick her up or be bothered with her until I picked her up and brought her home an hour and a half later.

My daughter recounted a story to me about a conversation with her Uncle Moe. When she was an adult, they went out for a drink one night and she started asking him questions about what he saw that occurred in our house. He knew Tim had a terrible temper and he actually saw him pound on Victor once in a while. He heard him scream at us and make us cry, but he never put it together. She asked him why he didn't force me to leave their father and why he didn't take Victor and her away from the house of terror. He said he never grasped the severity of our situation until he came to visit one night. Tim was in the garage in a rage, we had done something wrong, as usual. Uncle Moe came in and said hi then he was going to go into the garage and tease Tim as he always did. The sorrowful look on my face said it all; it will only make things worse for us if you do.

Later that night after Tim went to bed; I curled up next to my best friend and bawled my eyes out. I told him the horrible truth of our every day ongoing nightmare. Told him about the constant abuse and beatings that my son got, the put downs, the anguish of just breathing to survive and the steady fear we dealt with every second of each dark day. He had never known it was that bad. I hid the devastation, violence and cruelty so well; even from my best friend. Protecting the very person that should be exposed making sure none of the ugliness that lurks in our home spills out into the world for all to see. Over the years Uncle Moe and I talked many nights. I would leave a blue light on in the family room. He would know I was up and it was safe to come in. It was our secret signal to each other. Tim and the kids would be sleeping. We would sit there for hours talking. Most times he would put a reassuring arm around my shoulder and let me cry. Uncle Moe was always there for us no matter what the situation. He was a lifeline and a savior. He even caught me one day when I was putting up Christmas decorations. I was standing on a chair in the archway of the family room stretching up high to put up the lights. I over stepped the chair and went down. Uncle Moe had been sitting on the step below me watching and put his hands out and caught me in mid air. We looked at each other in shock and laughed. I knew without a doubt that I could and would always count on him in our lives. We would never cross the line; we were and still are best friends. I was married at the time and he was living with Jan. We both knew we could not hurt the other person. As miserable as it was for me I felt at the time it was my duty to stay married to the monster that I was hopelessly bound to. Little things, such as the mention of a video camera and not to own one, Tim had always wanted a camera. He said it would be great to be able to tape the children at family events. But I knew *without a doubt* that if we got a camera he would want to tape us in one of his many disgusting sex sessions. He had no respect for me and this would have been yet another degrading situation in my life. I will never own a video camera. Decorating cakes brings back to mind how he always had to put his fingerprint in each cake I made. Tim said it was his mark in the cake. He always joked about it but I knew it was another small way for him to remind me that he was in complete and total control at all times. I would have spent hours preparing and decorating a cake for someone, but he had no respect. He would just mark it his. This year for the first time since the children were born, they chose not to spend time with their father's family for the holidays. Both children say they are made to feel very uncomfortable by their paternal relatives and want nothing more to do with them.

Victor tells me all the time of the hatred he has for his father and how he would like to just once put his fist into his father's face. He tells of so many things that remind him of the countless beatings he received from his father. He also says that there is so much he has kept to himself and how it leaks out bit by bit. My son no longer speaks to his father. He went to the store to buy tires for his wife's car. The sales person asked if he was related to Tim standing behind the counter only a few short feet away. Victor said, "No he was not related to him and that he didn't know him." Victor then went around back to talk to a buddy of his and when asked if he talked to his father Victor said he no longer had a father. His father was standing about ten feet away and heard him. Tim said shit and walked away. Victor still has a lot of anger inside but he has learned to control it and has learned from his father's actions. He told me one day how scared Zoe was of him, because of his temper. Victor almost lost her that day and realized he had to be in control and treat this special woman with respect and decency if he wants his marriage to last. He knows that the control he has is over himself and his own actions and that he does not have to control his wife and everything around him. When the divorce first happened, my son took to eating as an outlet for his frustrations. The therapist said it was an *eating disorder* and it is one of many disorders that people use to comfort themselves. He put on at least 100 pounds, eating to console himself. No one else did, not even me. He doesn't realize that his weight can cause him many problems in the future. That he can become diabetic, have high blood pressure and have heart problems. But the worst of it is that he doesn't realize that he could lose the very thing most important to him and that is his beautiful wife and future family. If he doesn't get a hand on his weight he can die from being overweight and not be there for his precious wife and children in the future. Victor must come to terms with the fact that what he went through all those years **was not his fault**, but his father's fault. I am hopeful that once he deals with his own hidden secrets he will deal with his weight more effectively. Victor didn't seem to keep quite as much bottled up inside as his sister did. He took many of his frustrations out on the house and me, punching holes in the walls, destroying my things and being angry all the time. The one thing that really seems to bother my son is when his father calls and wants money from him. Victor owes money on a school loan that his father cosigned. Because of his financial situation he has not been able to pay it back of late. Victor keeps asking for the payment book, but has yet to receive it. Tim told Victor that he wanted the money to redo the kitchen and because he is getting a bigger motorcycle. Since the divorce Tim bought a house, a new truck, motorcycle, camper he only used once or twice, bought back the boat again from his sister, rebuilt and remodeled the upstairs to his house, put a new deck on the front and back of the house and still he wants more. Tim has not changed in my mind for he shows that material possessions and status are still what are important to him. He still wants control. Ever since Tim and Victor had the argument about the black truck, things have gotten worse between them. Victor told me that his father told his grandmother not to invite them to Easter dinner because he was upset and angry with them. So they were not invited. Still trying to control all he can. Marti called and asked if I heard from her brother but I didn't. She got a nasty message from her father telling her that he was through with her and her brother and that the two of them could go to hell. She and I both had no idea what was going on until I spoke with my son later that day. Victor had wanted to talk to his father about the money issue they were having and try to straighten things out between them. He also wanted to pick up his camping things that were stored at his father's house, but as always things escalated. They had a terrible argument on the phone which ended in them swearing at each other. Now again they were not talking to each other. Of course, it was all blamed on me. Tim told his son that once again I turned his children against him. After talking to Marti again, she said her father is still playing poor me. He went over to his mother's house the next morning suffering and saying he had not slept all night. That he was extremely upset by everything that occurs between himself, Victor and Marti.

It has been seven years since the divorce and still Tim and his family have not moved on. They still play the blame game. I started writing a journal before the divorce to help me deal with the turmoil, grief and the head games. It has taken me two years to tell of our atrocious journey of 19 years and still the games and abusiveness continue. This book has helped me tremendously to deal with what transpired over the years. However there are shocking events that still pop up once in a while. Such as while talking to my daughter on the phone she relayed to me the events of scouting. She recently remembers the events of scouting where she and her brother were not allowed to touch the refreshments at a function. She told me that her father forbid them to have anything stating that the food and drink were for the quests. Marti recalls me sneaking in cookies to her and Victor, because they had not eaten all day. For some reason this triggered a memory of my own. I remember many times Tim the children and I would be fooling around and he, once again, getting irate with us. I would then run around the living room through the kitchen and disappear down cellar. I would hide behind the furnace and Tim would not be able to find me. I would crouch down in the tiny space absolute darkness surrounding me holding my breath listening for him and ultimately I would hear him swearing, "Where the hell are you?" as he looked for me. He could never find me and I never told him of my hiding place even though he tried threatening me into telling him where it was.

28. Finally

Through the many years of abuse we survived. I cannot speak for my precious son and daughter for I know only part of what they feel and think. But, I do know that I can no longer be an injured party. Even though I cannot forgive what we lived through, and will never be able to totally forget, I can get past it. What the children and I endured for such a long time, I no longer want to carry around. In order not to be a victim any longer, I have to put aside all the hatred inside, the bitterness, anger, resentment, coldness, guilt and the heavy heart I carry with me every day. The demons and ghosts of the past must be put to rest. Marti said to me that she has guilt because she was the big sister and should have protected her brother, but that is not true. I first told her no, I was the mom and should have protected both of them and did not. But it wasn't because I didn't want to; it was because I could not protect them and because of the emotional circumstances in which we lived. The blame only lies with their father. He is the one that mistreated all of us. We were only in the line of fire waiting for the detonation of the bomb to go off. He is solely responsible for all we endured and he is the one who should own up to what he did. I will not accept the burden of his actions on my shoulders any longer. Even though there were a few good times, the abuse severely overshadows them, making it extremely hard to remember any of the good that did exist. Someone once said, "A bad back round isn't something to be ashamed of – it is something to overcome. " The toxic factors that poisoned our everyday life will not consume me any longer. Now, I want to try to live each day with dignity and not cower in the corner any more.

I know, I have personal and emotional problems still to deal with and by lightening my heart I can and I will for as my son said, "a bright light has shown, I don't have to run anymore because now love will always be there." I was strong then, but didn't know it and I am stronger now. I will keep getting stronger, because I know I am not alone in this fight against abuse. I know there are people out there who care and want to help. I will take one step at a time and do the best I can. Finally; the **signs were seen,** the voice inside spoke up and said **get out** before it is too late. And I knew with everything that was in my heart, the **most important** thing I had to do, was **keep us safe**.

~ *Epilogue* ~

The end. Those two little words... wishing, hoping and praying that they could be written down - but they cannot. The total devastation that took place for so many years will always creep back into the lives of the abused in one way or another. Screams in the night, flash backs, tears of repulsion and shocking memories will always remind us of those awful years we endured by a very abusive, sick, controlling person. The abuse, both physically and mentally to the children, as well as and the sexual abuse to myself will never completely go away. These memories lurk just beneath the surface, waiting for the most unsuspecting moment to emerge and wreak havoc once again. Yes, it will get easier in time, but the violent memories will always be there for us to struggle with. The children and I will continue to survive and deal with what is cast our way and we will continue to grow stronger and healthier each and every day. We know we have each other to count on and we know we have love with and for each other. Dealing with the circle of emotional ups and downs will continue for each of us in our own way.

Victor refuses to believe he needs counseling and believes that he is past his painful childhood. He wants to be able to talk with his father and just forget what transpired for so many years. It is my opinion that he is still in need of his father's approval and will always be searching for it in some way; I also believe his fuse is just below the surface and at some point in time it will finally ignite and explode. He says the past is in the past, forgotten and that is where it will stay. But Victor has told me of his need to protect me and his family and that he will always be there if needed. Victor and Zoe moved back to Oklahoma in October of 2007.

They had agreed to move to Massachusetts after getting married to start their lives together. Zoe, however, never got over being home sick. Once they found out she was expecting they knew it was time to go back to Oklahoma. In February of 2008 they had a beautiful little boy.

Marti is in counseling once again. This is her circle and how she deals with the terrible past. She starts counseling then stops when she gets too close to bad memories that she is unable to deal with. Each time she starts again, she moves a little further along. Marti knows she must keep a long distant relationship with her father. Their visits become explosive. Marti is also coming to terms with the abuse she endured. Her relationship with Timothy is finally over. She is starting to realize that she comes first and is taking action to improve herself and her life. She works in the administration department at school and has joined a gym. Marti has said, the swimming relieves a lot of the tension in her and helps with the migraine headaches she suffers from.

Maurice kept his word and took me to Hawaii for our 5th wedding anniversary. He has been a constant soft place for me to land and helping me when I take a step backward. He is also a good listener for the kids when needed. Marti and Victor have now accepted Maurice and whenever they see each other they say they love each other and give each other a hug.

As for myself, I have made the decision to move on knowing the monster (abusive behavior) is still out there; but I will be ready if I cross that path again. I take classes at the Network Against Domestic Abuse. The classes are very informative and I can relate to the material we go through. It is hard at times, but gives me a great understanding as to how I was manipulated and controlled for so many miserable years. The Network helped me tremendously through terrible times and now I want to give back. I felt so alone and in pain for such a long time. Now, I want people to know they are not alone and that there is hope and help. I help with fund raising events, serve as a volunteer for the Network on many projects and I have answered the crisis hot line. I want to learn as much as I can about Domestic Abuse so that I can continue to help spread the word that abuse in any form is *wrong*.

To all who read this book, I thank you for letting me share this story and ask that your heart be open to recognizing people like me. Victims look pretty normal and try to appear happy so that they can hide their shame. Pray for those recovering from abuse and listen and watch for the little signs of an abused person – maybe someone can offer to listen and encourage people to get help and support. October is Domestic Abuse awareness month; we wear purple ribbons to show support for the victims and survivors of abuse and try to make people more aware of the ongoing abuse that takes place every minute of every day. The National Violence Hotline number is 800-799-SAFE (7233), or www.ndvh.org/. The on-call staff can refer you to a local chapter for help.

STAY SAFE

~~~~~~~

Marianne Mooney was born and raised in Connecticut. She has two grown children and a grandson. After struggling through 19 years of an abusive marriage, she divorced and started the long journey to recovery. During this period she met a man who was a good friend to her, and who, eventually, became her husband. They have been married for seven years and live in Connecticut near their families.